UNCOMMON PRAYERS TO MOTHER MARY

UNCOMMON PRAYERS
to MOTHER MARY
365 prayers for daily inspiration & strength

Jennifer Clarke

Books by the author

Thru My Eyes and in My Words
What a Pain!
Thru My Eyes and in My Words Too
Conversations With Mary

Published 2021

© 2021 Jennifer Clarke

All images in this book are copyright Jennifer Clarke
jenclarke58@bigpond.com

Book design by Paper Horse Design & Publishing

ISBN 978-0-9925877-4-1

 A catalogue record for this book is available from the National Library of Australia

Cover painting © 2021 Carol Avery

To humanity and our future

About the cover

When I was much younger I could not relate to the image that the Church presented as the vision of Mother Mary. It was so European. So I pictured my own vision in my mind. I asked my friend Carol Avery to bring it to life. The cover of this book is the result.

—*Jennifer*

'I just love watercolour painting and sharing the joy!
I have rediscovered watercolour painting after many decades of life getting in the way, and am largely self-taught over the last couple of years.
If my painting draws you and holds your attention for a while; if it inspires you to create or attach your own stories to the art, then my work is done.'

—*Carol Avery*

Introduction

Back in early May 2020, I had a vision for this project slip its way into my mind. The vision was a request to write prayers to Mother Mary. I was asked to do this every day for twelve months. To say that I was somewhat confused then quickly aghast at the scope of the project sums it up quite well. After some creative verbal comments, including some amazing statements regarding my mental health status, I succumbed to the request.

Why this project? As I said, I was baffled! It was no simple task. I just sat there wondering how in Mary's name I was going to write 365 prayers that didn't end up being similar. It is truly a Faith project!

During the first draft I asked: 'Will I ever share this project with others?' I honestly didn't know at the time. I could not see much (literary) interest from anyone, except maybe some people who have a devotion to Mary. For some reason I was compelled to continue this exercise, and to find an answer to why this project had been given to me!

Well, I found one part of the answer very quickly when I shared my bafflement of the project with some friends and family. Their response was fascination and a request for a copy of the finished product.

So, here I am writing the introduction for *Uncommon Prayers to Mother Mary*.

Who is Mary to me? Mary has been an inspiration all my life. The Mary of my mind is a forthright woman whose strength of faith has echoed down through the centuries. To me she is comfortable with herself, her culture and her Faith. The Mary of my heart is not the white European woman as displayed in western church icons.

She is no wilting flower but vibrantly alive. In a patriarchal society she stands strong and honourably. To have been the mother of Jesus she would have been all these things. But she was not just a mother. She was also an individual who had a life of her own.

I am thinking that this, besides being a Faith project, will be a reflective personal observational exercise for me. I have been finding that as the days and months have passed there have been tendrils of thought that for no known reason whisper through my mind, and amazingly give me a direction for that day's prayer. Sometimes my mind wanders to something that happened the previous day, which then has my pen racing across the page.

At times the nature outside my back window has given me an obvious hint as to the structure of the prayer that morning. *If I look at nature closely enough there is always something happening.*

And then there was the one-word prayer, 'Help!' that did not make it to these pages but has definitely played a part in these 'Uncommon Prayers'. That part was when I was bereft of thought or ideas. It was at this point I realised that I might be the writer but in many cases Mother Mary was and is the inspiration. Here is an answer to those who ask: 'Are your prayers ever answered?' This project is but one example.

One of my concerns during this time was that the prayers would begin to take on a sameness. I read about seventy of the prayers to discover that only six had similar subject matter, and even where there was some similarity, each prayer had been written while I was in a different space, thus each had a different slant. One thing that did amuse me was that two of the prayers spoke about weeds…uncommon indeed!

Over time my prayers have become more like reflections with a prayer attached. In doing that I have opened up more of my personal truth to you. This makes me rather nervous as it is challenging to open myself in this way.

What benefit will this project bring me? My mind immediately fires back a question—does a Faith project need a benefit? In thinking about both these questions, I believe that this exercise will help me develop a stronger Faith and deepen my spiritual relationship with Mary. I also hope that you and I may gain some personal insight from my ramblings.

On the reflective, creative side, I have no doubt that that it will hone my skills by improving my centeredness, sharpen my visual and observational acuity, and focus my thought processes.

All of these answers are what will help to motivate me if, or should I say when, I become a little bogged in the project.

What is the meaning of prayer in my life? Firstly, it is acknowledgement of the presence of a Power greater than my own in my life. Without that acknowledgement prayer would be meaningless. It is also the acceptance that I am not an island and at times I do need help; that acceptance can be a hard one for me. Ironically, I have often prayed for this assistance during the year.

So, prayer is an acknowledgement of my Faith. If some prayer is about asking for assistance in some way, do I think that it is going to be granted? Prayer is several things for me but simply yes, prayers can be answered but not always in the way that I would like. As for the answered prayer—I sometimes call these miracles.

To me, prayer is also a conversation with the Divine. It is not about me asking and receiving what I request on a silver platter. I think that it is about discovering what my needs are and finding the strength within myself to achieve them. That is what the power of prayer does for me … it gives me the strength to believe in myself—and sometimes in those miracles.

I also think prayer is more than discovering what my needs are: It is about discovering me.

And I will never ever forget the prayer of thanksgiving. Why is this? It is to do not just with politeness. It is more than words. It is an acknowledgement from me, my heart and my Soul that I have not walked my life path by myself. I have gained strength to achieve and to become who I am today through this Power that is greater than myself. This Power is a part of my Faith journey. To me this deserves acknowledgement and thanks.

Prayer is the glue and communication of that journey: from unthinking prayer said by rote, to the meditativeness of my family's beloved rosary, to the creative original prayers of today. It has always been there, helping me in my Faith and my personal journey … my rock; my anchor.

Prayer is also the glue that has helped this project reach its conclusion. As I said earlier, 'I might be the writer but in many cases Mother Mary was and is the inspiration'. Without Mother Mary's guiding hand, I believe that many of these prayers would have been left unsaid and this project would have remained unfinished. I consider this project a team effort and thank Mother Mary for her input.

Now my mind moves to another type of prayer that I have rarely thought of. Whilst many a prayer is a request for assistance for self, others or a project, I have not often thought of those that I am praying to and what they may need. Have I ever asked: 'Is there anything that I can do for you?'

Deep within my Soul, I believe that I have found there the full answer to 'Why this project?' And that is to create prayers with a modern-day slant... ones that hopefully we all can relate to. If just one person gains insight or has their Faith strengthened, then this project has achieved its goal.

How to use this book? Any way you wish. To make it easier, there is an Index at the back which may help if you are looking for a specific prayer.

You still may not find the prayer that you are looking for. This leads me to my next project, which has been brought to you by my silent partner. If you do not find the prayer you seek and have decided that you cannot create your own, please contact me on jenclarke58@bigpond.com and I will write you one. My only request is that you make a small donation to a charity of your choice.

Finally, my prayer today is to you—that you find joy and strength in your heart as you walk the path of wherever these words take you. Amen.

Well, that is it for the Introduction. I will begin this project with the first prayer that I ever wrote to Mother Mary—My Lady's Prayer.

My Lady's Prayer

Lady Mary, I sit here aspiring to silence knowing that I need no words but an open heart to be within your spiritual presence.

I pray your example gives me the strength to search for my truth; to slow down and examine myself when I have stumbled or fallen into another of life's potholes.

I pray for guidance to understand the stumble and the strength to pull myself out of the pothole—or the humility to ask for help if I need it.

I pray for the energy and generosity of spirit that will have me stretching out my hand to whomever may be in need of that hand.

Please give me the grace to be patient with all the niggles of the day and the wisdom to understand that another's path I cross might not be so smooth at the moment it crosses mine.

Mother Mary grant me the wisdom to decipher my life experiences; to see and enjoy the beauty of life and creation that is all around me.

Teach me to be humble…I do know that miracles have been known to happen! So, I will continue to pray for the wisdom and gifts that do not come to me easily.

Amen.

All prayers start with Mother Mary...

May

Road in Western NSW

1 **Life does not have to be perfect for us to enjoy it. It is by its very imperfectness that we learn about who we are. I pray to you for the wisdom and strength that I need to accept myself for who I am and am becoming.**

2 One of the saddest things in the world today is the violence perpetrated within families, especially on the children. This violence harms all, not just the young who need and deserve our love. I know not where all the hate comes from but I pray to you for all children; that society will find a way to overcome all poverty and violence in the world. I pray to you for families; that the cohesive force of love within families will help children walk their life paths to their fullest potential. I also pray that all kids get to play freely throughout their childhood and that as we become adults we do not forget the child within.

3 Patience is a skill that I will spend the rest of my life working on. My lack of it at times can be teeth-grindingly frustrating. I know that preparation and attitude can be part of the answer but in my case it does not always succeed. I pray to you that when I begin to feel impatient, I spiritually take your hand and envision peace and calm coming to rest within my being. I thank you for your presence in my life.

4 Have I ever walked through the day and not noted anything beautiful, including the people around me? If so, then I must be blind. I pray to you that I find the sight to spend this day in awe of the world.

5 I cannot begin to count the number of times that I have faced disappointment in my life. And guess what? I survived all of them! What does that tell me? I pray to you that the next time I face disappointment, I think of this statistic and get a grip on the reality that is my life!

6 How many times have any of us ever said 'one day I'll get to that'? How often does that 'one day' happen? I thank you for helping me set goals in my life, to find a way to make the 'one day' happen more often. I pray to you that I will always be able to find the strength and courage to take the first step on a new path.

7 We all have different personality types. I have a personality type that is rather addictive. I was addicted to smoking for nearly forty years and it was one of the most difficult things in my life to give it up. I still have an addictive personality, I will until the day I die. I pray to you for all those who have an addiction of any kind, including myself, that we will find the strength within ourselves to get to the point where we can stop using that addictive substance; to find the freedom to release ourselves from the prison of dependence and then walk the path into our deeper potential.

8 Sometimes I need to close my eyes to improve my concentration. I work on becoming more centred so that I am able to access thoughts that may be wanting to surface. I pray to you to gently push me to practice my meditative skills daily, while at the same time praying for all who live on the face of this beautiful planet.

9 As we get older our minds—and sometimes our conversations—turn to not so much the *fact* that we are gonna die but *how* it may happen. As the years pass, we more and more become bystanders in the deaths of loved ones, be they friend or family. Some of those deaths are gentle, some are stripped of their dignity and for some it is a struggle to the final breath. One of my fears is developing dementia and having my final few years taken from me by confusion and memory loss. I pray to you that my final journey is one that I face with acceptance and dignity; that I spend it in joy and thanksgiving for all that I received in life and the knowledge that I have gained. Thank you for what I have received so far.

10 I am not sure if any scientific study has been done on the correlation between a cloudy sky and being somewhat depressed. I know that when I am feeling a little down on a cloudy day, I sit in a chair facing the window, I take some deep breaths and slow down mentally. I then visualise myself floating through the beautiful fluffy clouds until I can feel the sun on my face again. I pray to you to assist me to envision my trip through the clouds and, like the wind, help me to blow my sadness away.

11 Some people seem to live their lives looking behind themselves into their past. I've even heard people say that school was the best years of their life. I sit and wonder how someone is able to live in the present happily when they think their best years are behind them. I pray to you that those who feel this even a tiny bit are able to find ways to set goals for themselves so that they can live meaningfully in the present and even look forward to what the future may hold.

12 Is it the finding of the answer to the question that is most important, or is it in the asking of the question? For me, the asking is what leads me onto the path of inquiry so I will always say that it is the journey not so much the answer. Although, for my sanity, I would like to find an answer or two. I pray to you that I will always find you on the journey and that the journey will help strengthen my faith and self-awareness.

13 One of my biggest difficulties can be the acceptance of compliments. Some are humble in their acceptance of praise; some believe it is their due; and some do not think that they deserve it. In my book all are worthy of praise no matter their achievements. I pray to you that each of us will honour the compliment that is given to us. It is a gift of truth and should be accepted as such. I should always be gracious in that acceptance.

14 I saw a falling star last night and it brought a smile of childish delight to my face. For when I was a child a falling star was one of the times that I would dream of magical moments. For me this was a time of childhood innocence. I could be cynical in my adulthood and just say that it is just another piece of space junk coming to earth. But I do not wish to be cynical as this fleeting childhood moment was a happy memory for me. I pray to you that in difficult adult times I am able think of the joy of this memory; and that joy will bring me the strength to walk away from any present angst.

15 'They' say that you can choose your friends but you cannot choose your family. This is most often said in jest but unfortunately often has feelings of bitterness attached. Sometimes we think that we don't have to work on family relationships just because they are family. Sadly, we also seem to take family for granted, but in so doing deny the truth. It is in the cauldron of our early family experiences that our personalities are forged. Some of those experiences were painful. I pray to you to help me remember that every single member of my family, no matter their gender or generation, has suffered at times through their childhood. I pray that we find within us the compassion to acknowledge this truth, and find the strength to stand beside our loved ones in forgiveness.

16 Without a doubt, fear is a great way of limiting my creative potential. Fear might slow me down but I just have to look at what I have achieved in my past to know that what I may be facing in my future is a definite possibility. I reckon that my first ever challenge would have been learning how to walk and since then I have been moving into my future one step at a time, sometimes struggling to make headway, sometimes tripping over obstacles, sometimes even side-lined. And then there are the times when I have had the joy of running … wow! I pray to you that when I do feel fear, you help me to visualise you standing beside me supporting me with your strength so that instead of tripping over my own two feet I will remember how to run.

17 I looked out on the horizon this morning and I saw smoke. My first thought was that this was a harbinger of things to come even though I knew there must have been some burning off yesterday to cause the smoke. So I look at the smoke now and see two things—preparation for an increase in the heat and memories of last year's disaster. I pray to you that we all learn from what happened last year; that those most affected have found healing; and that summer will be kind to all this season.

18 Sometimes we can try too hard; sometimes we do not achieve what we set out to do. Sometimes we fall into life's potholes; sometimes we have to stop, through no fault of our own, and sometimes we see all of this as a failure. And we'd be wrong. What I see as a failure is not trying at all. For me, life is about three things—getting to know myself, finding and working with my potential and having fun while I am doing it. Potential can change because of age, experience and illness. So, in a sense I am forever redefining myself. I pray to you that as my life progresses, I find the courage to continue to explore who I am and find ways to express myself that I never thought possible.

19 Have you ever looked at someone and wondered what they were about? We all have idiosyncrasies that others may find difficult to interpret or understand. How accepting and respectful am I of these personalities? Were they bullied as children; ignored as possible friends; or even whispered about in derogatory terms? How hard do I find it to accept these people who walk their own authentic path? We all have a right to be ourselves and yet, many of us can find it difficult to give another the right to be themselves. I pray to you that I always find within myself the respect for all, however they portray themselves; and that I acknowledge the right of all to travel their own unique journey.

20 One thing that I have noticed about lifestyles through the many, many years that the human race has existed (and no, I have not lived that long—I've just watched documentaries!) was the apparent need for us to acquire possessions. In this generation, that need has increased exponentially. And then there are those who live a simple life with much fewer possessions. There is something attractive about their lifestyle. Unfortunately, I have sometimes believed that I need my possessions to have a happy life. I do not need possessions to see beauty; to understand myself, to love, to enjoy another's company or be comfortable (How comfortable do I need to be?). I don't need possessions to give my life meaning. I pray to you that I might only possess what I need to live comfortably; that I give away that which I don't need nor makes me happy; and that I challenge myself when I am about to make a purchase. Do I really need it? Challenging, hey!

21 For those who think and do use violence in any form as the answer to an issue that they may be facing; I pray that in the future they find a peaceful way to resolve their problem/s. Help us all to choose wisely the paths we must take in life.

22 I might think that I can see in the dark but it is not until I can see in the full light of day that I will know more truth. I pray to you for enlightenment for all of humanity during these troubled times. Grant us all the strength to find the patience we need to experience the fullness of life.

23 The longer I stay in the one spot I reckon the more that I would see. But then again, it depends on my focus. I might be standing in front of a spectacular view but, if my mind is elsewhere, the chances of me later describing the full view are pretty slim. I pray to you that when I am in the moment, I stay there, so that I am fully able to experience all that moment has to offer.

24 I wonder if a person's imagination could be deleted from their potential, simply by denying that person a view of their world from a very early age? What a dreadful thought. To me, without imagination I am a prisoner in my own mind. My creativity would have never come to fruition. I pray to you that we all find ways to open each other's minds, so that our imagination can blossom with the joy, enlightenment and enrichment of and for all.

25 We all suffer in many and unique ways, whether that be physical, emotional or mental. Sometimes the road to our futures is littered with potholes and corrugations that just cannot be avoided no matter how hard we try. As a result of our all too human sufferings, we often cross paths with those who are doing it just as tough, and at times even more so. In my own pain and exhaustion, it is almost impossible to make allowances for another's need. I pray to you that I find within myself the grace to respect another's painful journey. I also pray for the strength to rise above the frustration of my own suffering and not take it out on others.

26 Depression is something that we all suffer from at some point in our lives. It can be baffling and scary. When I am feeling down, I feel like I have little control over my life. I pray to you that I am able to find ways that bring me joy; that when I am most out of control, I look within myself to find the strength and understanding to give the depression a good swift kick. I know that depression is not that easy to shift but I pray that I continue to look for positive ways to move it out of my life; and that when the times get too tough, to remind myself that it is okay to ask for help.

27 It is my belief that one of my/our responsibilities in life is to help people see that they have something to offer society; that their life truly has meaning. There are a lot of people in our society who feel that they have lost their way; that they cannot discover the potential that they possess. I pray to you that we—as individuals and as a society—discover a way to help people participate positively and creatively in life.

28 There is one day every year that I take the time to reflect on how special and unique that I am. It is also a day of thanksgiving for all that I have been given in life. I pray to you with thanks for the potential that I have been gifted with throughout my life. I thank you for the joy and for the love. I also pray that all will be blessed with the gift of healing on their special day.

29 One of the hardest things in life is to honestly share how I am feeling with others, be it about how I am hurting, the way someone treated me or just about distressed feelings I may have. Sometimes it's about protecting myself. How often do any of us share our true/deepest feelings or thoughts with anyone? I pray to you that in the future you help me find the courage to share myself honestly with others.

30 There are many different names for humans. One of the names that would not often be used, but I think is a valid choice is 'sufferer'. We suffer through childbirth. We suffer through growth. We suffer through puberty. We suffer through illness and disease. We suffer through change. We suffer through loss. We suffer through life. We suffer on the road to death. And if someone does not think that the person that they are looking at has no courage then I ask you to look again. Anyone who is human has courage just by walking into their future. I pray to you that all of us begin to understand that while each of us travels a different path, we all travel a path that is similar … courage, pain and suffering are just part of the baggage we all carry, though some carry a heavier load than others. So before we decide to judge another person, take time to realise and respect each other's truth. I also pray that we all learn compassion for our companion travellers.

31 I am sure that all of us have at some point in our lives had a serendipitous event happen, a coincidence, if you will. For me this can be a sign to focus; a sign that something is happening or going to happen that I will learn from. It may even point me in a direction that I need to take. I pray to you that, during these times, I have the awareness to pay particular attention, to work on discovering what it means for me.

June

A young cousin camp drafting at Gladstone

32 Life is not just about work and being totally serious. It is also about having fun and enjoying life. In my opinion, life without smiling is just not living. I pray to you to help us find the clown within ourselves, and in each other, and that we might honour and nurture this essential gift.

33 It is often difficult to believe in something, especially if you have not seen it or you do not know the person who told the story. Why is it so hard for us to believe the truth? There are so many untruths out there and we all know that we sometimes lie to protect ourselves—well, I know that I have! I pray to you that I find the courage to speak from the heart and that I honour myself by speaking the truth.

34 I reckon that time is our most precious commodity. I pray to you that we all use it wisely to our own benefit and in service to the rest of humanity.

35 If we are going to make a noise, make it joyful and strong. I pray to you that all those who have a voice use it wisely and for the betterment of all.

36 When I see those living in squalor, the hungry and homeless, besides it being a failure of society, I personally feel like a failure. And that is as it should be. This blight is not just the responsibility of governments, it is our responsibility. I pray to you that I personally find a way to reach out my hand. I individually cannot solve the problem but when many hands are stretched out in help, then the world becomes better bit by bit. I also pray that the equality of human resources quickly becomes a major goal of all governments and peoples around the world.

37 I look at the beauty that is around me and think of those living in a poverty of spirit. I pray to you that they realise that they have been touched by a power greater than themselves. I also pray that their eyes are opened to their potential within.

38 I pray to you that we all come to an understanding of the preciousness and potential of all life.

39 When I think I am owed an apology I must make sure that I know and accept the truth first. I pray to you that when I am angry with another, I pause and consider my words before letting loose.

40 For those who wish to share their misery with another, I pray to you that they stop and think about how bad they are feeling. I pray that we all find the strength to share our thoughts, not pass on our pain.

41 I thank you for the strength to speak my truth. I pray that I can turn to you when I need understanding, and the weight of anger and resentment removed from my life.

42 I pray to you for those who feel and believe that life owes them. I also pray that all of our eyes are opened to the greater needs, poverty and pain that surrounds us in all parts of the world.

43 When I look at the birds in the sky I notice that each different species has a distinctive way of flying. For each of them it gets the job done. Although humans cannot fly, each of us is an individual. I pray to you that we all give each other the freedom to express ourselves in our own unique way.

44 When I see a frog from the inside of a window that is what I think of when I hear the word sucker. Every part of their webbed feet is attached to the glass. I pray to you that as I live life, I become as totally attached and focused on the goals that I aim for.

45 When I see a tear track down someone's face I mostly believe that they are tears of grief and sadness. Rarely when I see tears do I think of joy. I pray to you that we all find ways to help heal the tears of sadness in the world, and turn those tears to ones of joy and openness and care.

46 We have only a finite amount of time on this planet. I pray to you that we all find ways to use that time wisely, including bringing self-knowledge into our daily lives. I also pray that we find joy in the journey.

47 When I think about something that I would love to do but cannot, I feel a little like my hands are tied behind my back. I can envision doing a drawing in my mind but when I try to enact that vision I am no better than a young child drawing stick figures. I pray to you, as I continue my journey through life, that with your guidance I discover the creativity within myself, and grow more proficient in nurturing the creativity I now have.

48 When I am at the beach I go to this one particular spot to try and shoot a perfect image of a wave as it is about to break. In the last several years, I've taken about 20,000 photos in the one spot. I've kept only about 200 of them. A few of the images are quite good but none of them are the perfect wave as I see it. If I was to define patience in my life this activity would be it. It is the one spot where I can honestly say that I have patience. If you were to ask about the rest of my life I would say my record would be miserable. I pray that in the future I take the skills that I have gained in this part of my life and use them as an example for the rest of my life. I've shown that I have the motivation and ability …now use it!

49 I woke this morning to a picture of a perfect day. The birds were singing. The horses, cows and, much to the disappointment of the farmers, the 'roos were feeding peacefully in the paddocks. My thought was the question: What can I achieve today, and will I learn anything new? For all of those who do not see hope at the beginning of a new day, but boredom and drudgery, I pray that they will find meaning in their lives; that they are able to access their potential, and share that potential with others around them who may be in need of hope also.

50 There are times when I have no control over my life. This can scare me. I pray to you that I will find the strength and Faith within myself to accept my present path and to learn from the fear and loss that I may experience.

51 I pray to you that we all find some time to watch children play. Their joy in living is infectious; their simplicity, compassion and honesty has a lot to teach us. I also pray that their activities will take us back in our memories to a time when we played. Gift the children and the child within us our precious time.

52 When I arise I take time to appreciate the softness of the early morning, with the joy of the birds singing as they greet the dawn. I pray that I welcome the morning like this every day, and give thanks for the gift of who I am and for the people in my life.

53 I consider one of the hardest things in life is to not immediately judge a book by its cover. I pray to you to help me help those in need by accessing the compassion and insight I have within, and to offer my hand in a way that honours and treats the other person with respect.

54 Many memories can be found in the people we know; in our possessions, the view or a news story; in the food we eat or even a smell. These memories are a part of my history, who I am and how I got where I am now. I pray that I wisely use these memory tools to guide me on my journey of self-discovery and Faith.

55 I sit here inspired by the magnificence of creation, with the incredible diversity of animals that inhabit this beautiful land. I pray to you that we all learn to respect and understand the balance between living thoughtfully within the environment and the selfless use of its resources.

56 I stood and looked at the ocean today. The sky was brilliantly blue and the sun was gently warm. It was a beautiful day but I had to grumble that the sea was flat. I pray to you that I might overcome this 'nothing is quite good enough' attitude, and accept with graciousness my reality. I also pray with humble thanks for all that I do have.

57 It is an interesting activity and also worth discovering the roots of our ancestry. Some of us may not be proud of what we find but I do know that our ancestor's journey is not our responsibility. I pray to you that we learn by example from each other's paths as we work and walk to make our paths uniquely our own.

58 Loneliness is very hard for those who live with it constantly; aloneness is a gift that many seek when they need time to themselves. The difference can be choice, but often loneliness can be to do with life circumstances. To me loneliness saddens the soul and takes away from the beauty of living. For me alone time brightens the soul and opens my eyes to the wonder of life. I pray to you that we find ways to walk away from our loneliness and that, when we find those who are lonely, we share our precious time with them.

59 There are many that would argue robustly that the sky is blue. Their minds could not be changed until you stood with them under a morning or evening sky. Many of us will not believe until we have seen it for ourselves. I pray to you that I am open to believing in the truth, even if I cannot see it, and that I trust the truth of those around me. My truth is not the only truth!

60 When I was a child the people in the bush often did not have access to equipment to build and engineer the roads that they travelled. They often had to forge their own roads by going over the same ground over and over. When there was a rough piece of track usually caused by runoff from rain there would be several sets of tracks forged in an attempt to find the smoothest path. I pray to you for guidance that when my path is rough I can find the right and smoothest path for me at that time. I also pray for the strength and perseverance while journeying through those rough spots.

61 No matter our culture, country, gender, religion or just plain difference, we are all uniquely individual. I pray to you that each of us respects our differences, and that we all help each other walk the paths of our own choosing.

July

West Kempsey at sunrise

62 When I start a project I feel a varying degree of nervousness as to my ability to finish the project. The degree of nerves depends on how challenged and discomforted I am. I pray to you that at these times I find the faith I need to believe in myself and that I take time to contemplate the memories of previous achievements. I also pray that I find the strength to not rest on my laurels, but continue to challenge myself to step outside my comfort zone.

63 I can sit inside my warm home with my heater on in my warm cloths and exclaim at how cold it is outside. How often do I send thanks for being one of the lucky ones who lives in warmth. Or do

I think that I achieved this warmth all by myself? I pray to you that, in times when I am warm and it is cold outside, I remember those who are homeless, who are in war-torn countries or who are poor and cannot afford heating. I pray that I do not even have to feel the cold to find a way within my means to help those neighbours in need. In Mother Mary's book everyone is a neighbour!

64 I look into the sky and I see the moon setting. But for a few degrees of separation all of humanity can see the same sight. All of humanity walk, crawl or wheel on the same planet, except we do it in different hemispheres. We all drink water provided from this earth. We all breathe its air. No matter who we are, where we come from, our cultural, religious or social status, we are all custodians of this planet. I pray to you that we all feel this awesome responsibility and do our best for Mother Earth; that we all remember how to give and not just to take.

65 At times I find myself a slave to my emotions. I can sometimes lose my temper at the simplest of things. I pray to you that I continue to look for ways to keep my balance, so that I do not succumb to negative emotions that can damage; that I find my peace and share that peace with others around me.

66 It doesn't matter how small the donated item may be … $1; ten minutes of your time; giving old clothes or whitegoods. You are giving within your means and it shows a generosity of spirit. It is the giving that counts. I pray to you that we all work on strengthening our generosity by looking for ways in which we can help our sisters and brothers.

67 There are times when I rush around like one of those wind-up toys, like a tightly wound clock, forever worried I'll run out of time. I pray to you that I can continue to learn how to live in the moment and discover new ways to be comfortable in my own company; to see the times I have with others as an opportunity to enjoy and learn more about me and my life.

68 When I put others on a pedestal I need to make sure that the pedestal is built on reality. I should ask myself the question—is this person worthy of the honour of being placed there? I pray to you that those who aim to live a life of faith and goodness look to you as a stunning example of that life.

69 'They' say that every cloud has a silver lining. There speaks an optimist. More often there are gloomy predictions of driving rain followed by floods. I pray to you that I find the direction to forever walk the path of the optimist and that I continually look for the silver lining in my day.

70 I need to trust that what happened to me today is meant to happen. Would I have trusted that statement when I was injured? Probably not! Every single one of us has rough and 'why me' moments in our lives. I pray to you that I continue to accept my path in life and that I acknowledge and help in any way I can those whose lives are so much more challenging; and that I continue to ask the question, 'why not me'?

71 Friendship is one of the most precious gifts we can be given on our journey through life. The many gifts that it brings to me include companionship, joy, a reminder of childhood, belonging, moral guidance and healing. I pray to you that I never take my friends for granted and that I gift them the way that they have gifted me; that I will become a better person and know myself more because of their presence in my life. Thank you for the gift of my friends.

72 I look to the sky this morning and I see the birds wheeling in all directions. To me it looks a little like they do not know where they are going. I sometimes feel the same about my own or another's path. I pray to you that I learn to trust the path that I walk is the right one for me at this time; that I do not judge the rightness of another's path. Their life is not for me to judge.

73 There is such joy in discovering there is something new that I can do. The journey to get me to the point of even trying can be most amazing. I pray to you that when something happens in my life that I do not understand help me to take the time to reflect on its meaning and how it may affect me into the future.

74 I sit here thinking that today is going to be a failure; that I won't be able to find a prayer because I am not centred enough; that this will be my first cry for help. I pray to you that I will learn to sing like the morning birds and those that glide seemingly effortlessly upon the wind; that I will continue to re-learn that I am not a failure and that memories will no longer have power over my life. Can you please help me to focus better on my centre and to live in the moment? Thank you.

75 Whether we dream big or small the most important thing to start with is that we believe in ourselves, because when we do, anything is possible. I pray to you that I find within myself the ability to fully believe in me; that I abolish those negative thoughts that can lead to expectations of failure.

76 I believe that there is no such thing as a poor or bad prayer. I pray to you that when I am without words, you will still hear my thoughts. Thank you for your care.

77 When I am weak I can lie to protect or enhance myself to others. I pray to you that I will find the strength to walk into my future accepting the truth of who I am.

78 Families come in all shapes and sizes. What should glue them all together is love and respect for each member of that family whether they be heart or blood family. I pray to you that we all take responsibility for the love that we have for each other; that we respect each other's journey in life; that we learn the give and take that is a part of all relationships.

79 I dislike not being able to see fully. It is like living with a fog over my eyes. I pray to you that I will find the healing and knowledge that will clear my sight so that I can see more of the truth.

80 Why is it that I sometimes tend to think of negative instead of positive outcomes? I pray to you that I will find wisdom, walking into the future with the Son shining in my life rather than the thought of a possible gloomy failure.

81 We all come in different shapes, sizes and colouring. We all dress differently. Some are more attractive than others. I pray to you that when I meet a person for the first time, I look for the person within, remembering that the true personality can sometimes take time to shine.

82 Emptying our minds of thoughts can be a difficult exercise. Following a stubborn thought can lead to an enlightening experience. I pray to you that I continue to take the time to listen to myself; to focus on daily activities that may teach me more about who I am.

83 When I am feeling down there is nothing worse than being in the same room as someone who is bright and chirpy. At these times I don't feel very Christian. I pray to you that when I am feeling this way, I do not take my bad mood out on others, but work to find joy within myself and appreciate the beauty of life around me.

84 Being frozen in fear can be mistaken for courage; our emotions sometimes become confused. It is not what I feel that is important, it is how I respond. I pray to you for the inner strength to overcome whatever emotion I may feel, so as to achieve an outcome worthy of my spirit.

85 There are times when my faith is weak and I question my path. I luckily live in a country that prides itself on personal freedom, giving me the freedom to follow my Faith. When my Faith is strong, I see life more clearly. I pray to you that, during times of struggle, I remember the clarity of my life and the joy of the belief in my Faith.

86 Many of us sometimes wish that we were someone else, because we are either attracted to their way of life or the skills that they have, and we desire to have that same skill. This is a path that for me is untrue. I pray to you that we all work on travelling our own authentic path; that we don't make copies of ourselves by trying to copy someone else's life. I pray that we are given the vision to see ourselves as we truly are and that moves us on our own genuine path.

87 Have I ever felt that the world owes me? Have I come across a line of people wanting to be served in some way? Have I felt better than them? Have I wanted to push those in the line out of the way because I believed at the time that my needs were more important than anybody else's? This attitude is one of arrogance; superiority. Whenever I feel this I can guarantee that I am on the wrong path. I pray to you to help me to realise the truth, that I might work on rectifying and finding forgiveness for this wrong.

88 Sometimes, the path to our final breath can be more stressful the closer we come to the end of life. For some, this path is the most difficult one that we face. The thought of leaving our loved ones can bring us deep pain and loss before we have to face it. The fear of taking this final road alone after having journeyed closely together for many years with our loved ones creates a hole that cannot be filled. I pray to you that we all find a way to reach out in spirit; to hold that loved one in our heart and share the joy that love has brought to us in life, that has made our life more fulfilling. Mother Mary I thank you for the preciousness of all the love that I have in my life.

89 One of the greatest joys in life is going somewhere I have never been before. It can also be very challenging, depending on the way I look at it. Yesterday I drove up a road that I have never travelled. My destination was full of beautiful scenery and wildlife, but the journey brought me as much joy as it opened up a new vista at every turn. I pray to you that I have the courage to not only to go to new places but to face personal challenges that I have never faced before. I ask for your guidance when facing that which I'd rather step away from. For in facing the new is the only way I can learn more about myself and the world that I live in.

90 When I open my eyes of a morning one of my first thoughts is to review what I have planned for the day. I wonder by the end of that day how much that plan will have changed, either in an organised or messy way. Each day brings its own mystery. I pray to you that I continue to be flexible to possible change at any point in my day. Total control is not nor will it ever be possible.

I pray that I help ease any future frustration, by taking on board this flexibility in my life as a skill that I need to work on each day.

91 One thing that I have noted while being sick is that I can still see beauty while feeling miserable, although I have to say I don't enjoy it as much. I pray to you that, during the tough times, I try and take time to enjoy the good and beautiful in my life. If I am finding that too hard, I need to swallow my pride and ask for a little help.

92 Beauty is in the eye of the beholder. So are weeds. I was stumbling through the bush the other day and a friend bent down, picked up a leaf then gave it to me to eat, saying that I needed more greenery in my diet. I grumbled that a green jelly bean would have done it ... and tasted better too! I pray to you that I always take the time to look at what I might describe as weeds, and spend time finding the beauty within my relationships with friends and family. Wisdom can also be found in the so called weeds.

August

Mercy Cross, Grafton, NSW

93 No matter its format the prayer does not need to be creatively brilliant, just heartfelt. I believe there is no such thing as a bad prayer. For me what is sad is the one that is not said. I had a friend who was suffering from Dementia. One day she cried out in sorrow that she couldn't remember how to pray. With tears in my eyes I realised that I was honoured to hear the most moving prayer I had ever heard. I pray to you that you gently touch all of those who wish to pray, to help them to see that it

is the thought and the feelings not just the words that make the prayer.

94   There are times when I push myself too hard and I end up exhausted. I often make wrong choices because of it. Sometimes it is important to stop and let life pass me by while I take that time to regain my strength. I pray to you that I will always recognise this point in my life; that I will take the time to regenerate; and acknowledge that others also need and deserve this time.

95   I do not have to be seen to be a presence in another's life. Like the wind that cannot be seen but can be felt through a gentle breeze or a disastrous storm, so are our relationships with others. I pray to you that I am a respectful and, if needed, healing presence in the lives of those around me; with a touch of humour on the side. A smile in today's landscape is about the only infectious part of humanity's make-up that I reckon we should not have a problem sharing!

96   No matter how beautiful the day is, when you are grieving life seems to have lost its shine. I pray to you for all those who have just stepped onto the path of grief, that there will be others with strength and compassion to be there to walk beside them, until life begins to matter again.

97   The beauty of the views outside my verandah window continue to shout my good fortune to me, no matter the state of my mind or body. I pray to you that I continue to see and give thanks for my good fortune in life.

98   Even heroes have heroes. There are people that we all look up to and admire; someone we might have liked to model our lives on. But we need to remember that not all heroes or famous people are a good influence. I pray to you for your guidance so that if I choose to admire someone who has caught my eye, I respect them for their human qualities and not just because they are famous.

99   In photography there are times when the capture of a brilliant image is more about good luck than good management. The best

image often is the one that was never taken, but just resides in the memory. I saw it but I was not ready. Life can be like that, when something that we think we are about to achieve slips through our fingers. I pray to you that when life happens like this, you help me to accept the present reality; help me to prepare for future possibilities and to ask for help if needed.

100 From the sublime, 'There is no way this is possible,' thought; to the ridiculous, 'This is easier than I believed and I am gonna rest on my laurels,' moment. Yes, my belief in my abilities can swing from one end of the pendulum to the other. From frustration at my inability to a touch of arrogance at what I have achieved. I pray to you that I continue to work on the balance in my own self-beliefs; that I take pride in my abilities by am also humble in my achievements.

101 Life is full of contrasts. Rough/smooth; good/bad; beautiful/plain; hot/cold; easy/hard. To me, contrasts are about understanding opposites. How could I understand happiness if I had not felt sadness? How could I be excited about an achievement that was hard if I had not experienced the easy? How could I not understand the strength of my Faith if I had not lived through the agony of doubt? I pray to you that I find the lessons and the positives in the contrasts of my life; that in using the contrasts they will light my path ahead.

102 Love is able to forgive a lot, but we should not take it for granted. Whether it be a new or old friend or family, love needs to be nurtured and cared for, but never abused. Love is one of the strongest elements on earth but it can be lost through abuse and disrespect. I pray to you that I hold this gift in my heart with gentleness, and for those who may harm love, help them to realise the damage that they can do.

103 'They' say that change can be as good as a holiday. I say that if you are not careful it can lead to stress and confusion. I pray to you that when there is change in my life, you help me to become clever enough to investigate that change and work on how it may affect me on my personal journey.

104 Those who have more money than others often spend their wealth on more luxuriant homes than others—larger building; higher in the hills; expensive suburbs; gated community. Good on them I say; I have to believe that they have earned their just rewards. I pray to you for help in not judging a book by its cover; that I relate to others by their deeds, not by what they own and wear.

105 A watched pot never boils, and an unwatched tap overflows a plugged sink quicker than you can say a naughty word. Where this prayer is going to, I have no idea, so I will just have to say that when I am confused in life, I pray for your help in finding the clarity and answers that I need.

106 I sometimes wish that I could use a scrubbing brush to wash away the emotions that make me feel sad and cranky. Usually I feel this way when I have no control over a certain issue. I pray to you that when I feel this way, I am reminded that another person's right to choose can sometimes affect me; be sad, be cranky for a while but acknowledge the rights of others to choose.

107 I looked out the window this morning, and the sky looked a little funny. My first thought was dirty fog, but then I took a closer look and realised that it was dust … dust from the land of those still suffering from drought. It is so easy to ignore those who are doing it tough when their plight is not in your face. I pray to you that we all become more aware of those who are having a rough time. Whatever we are able to do, I pray that we will always find ways to be generous to our neighbours whatever their need.

108 I sometimes look at life in such a way that has me thinking negative thoughts. An example—'Nothing is going to go right for me today.' I call these idiotic views 'self-prophesising rubbish'. I know that my life is never going to be perfect. I also know that I am going to find happiness and self-awareness in that imperfection. The more I think negatively, the less likely I will be happy. Yes, I know that there are going to be low points but I also know that I don't need to go looking for them. I pray to you that when I am feeling negative about life, you help me to look at life differently; to see the beauty in a scene, feel the calming heat of the sun upon my face or smile at the innocent laughter of children; to rejoice in an achievement; to enjoy the chirping of the birds; to delight in the visit from a loved one; and to be thankful at my path in life.

109 Spring is a season I look forward to with joy. I am one of those lucky people who do not suffer from hay fever, so I am happy when the earth warms and the first buds are starting to appear. This part of the planet is coming out of its hibernation and beginning to show its promise after so long waiting in the cold. I pray to you that we all take the time to nurture the potential within ourselves; that we find a way to fertilise that beauty and then take joy in watching that potential bloom.

110 Just because I cannot fly does not stop me from dreaming about flying. Just because I cannot paint does not stop me from picking up a brush and splashing colour around. Just because I cannot walk doesn't mean I cannot dream of running on the beach and feeling the sand between my toes. You see, dreaming for me is about visualising doing things I never thought I could do and finding ways to make them happen. Just because I cannot see the end of the road, does not mean I should not start on the journey. How many goals do I have on my 'kark-it' (bucket) list that I know are unachievable, or nearly so? I pray to you that I find the courage to dream about climbing hills and achieving things I never thought possible, and to believe that the impossible might just be achievable.

111 Why is it that some feel the need to hide their light? They do not stand out in any way; while some people have that look-at-me attitude; and then there are some people that are so balanced emotionally that they calmly journey through life happily content with their lot. I pray to you that we all find our right path in life, one that gives us the freedom to be ourselves and explore the beauty of life; a path where we feel comfortable and at home.

112 My goal in life is to know myself as fully as I am able. To achieve this knowledge and self-awareness I must develop and maintain skills in observation, focusing and reflection. I pray to you for the continual motivation to work on knowing myself fully, and that I use that knowledge to strengthen my faith and be the best person that I can.

113 As I get older and I start to forget a few simple things, my mind does not skip to the dreaded 'D' word automatically. Instead I see my mind as a somewhat out-of-date, though brilliant for its time, storage system that has been steadily stuffed with knowledge and memories since the day I landed in this part of the Milky Way Galaxy. It is understandable that sometimes it is slower to access the information that I require. I pray to you that as I get older, you give me a little reminder every so often that life is not about worrying about the future, it is about enjoying life no matter the hardship. Now that is a challenge, hey!

114 'They' say that misery loves company. I say that is a selfish attitude. I believe in offering sympathy to those in need but I also believe in keeping my misery to myself unless I am in need myself. I pray to you that I find a way of caring for myself without inflicting my own pain onto others, and that I am able to offer compassion without taking their misery on board.

115 How do you feel when someone says No to you? For me, it can be frustrating because it could affect my own personal plans. I sometimes even feel rejected. I have worked on saying 'No' to others, in a polite way, so that I could get the personal time that I needed. For many years, I have found it difficult to say 'No', as I am sure it has been for other people. It can be hard to disappoint others. I pray to you that when I am asked for some assistance, you help me to remember that it is important to have time for myself; please help me to be understanding and supportive when someone has to say 'No' to me.

116 How do I stand morally, if I have Faith and use prayer to help me achieve a positive outcome on a project that I am working on? Does the Lord or Mother Mary deserve recognition as part of a successful team? Or would I feel more comfortable if it goes without saying? Challenging, hey? In my heart of hearts, I believe that the Power that is greater than myself has played a part in engineering my creative skills. I pray to you that in future I find the strength and courage to stand by my Faith and acknowledge what I believe to be true—you are my partner in creativity and the soul of my Faith.

117 Can someone love me when I am always wearing masks? They would not really know who I am? I ask another question—What is love? Part of that for me is to be comfortable being totally myself with another. So another part of that is having the courage to let down those masks to show others my true self. Love is the most precious gift we can give or be given. I pray to you that we all find the courage that we need to be ourselves with those who wish to know us more, and those that we wish to know more.

118 Making the best out of a poor situation is something many have to face every day. When I get crabby about something that is not right, or not going the way I would like, I need to take a deep breath and think about how others may not have it anywhere near as good as I do. I pray to you that when I do get cranky, I take the time to consider my true reality; that is, that I am not doing it so tough. I also pray for those who are having a rough time of it, that they will find ways to travel a path that brings them more joy.

119 There are times when I do it tough. In past prayers I've talked about recognizing that others do it tougher. This time I wish to acknowledge and value my own unique journey; that even though someone may have a tougher path than I at this moment, it does not negate what I am going through now. I pray to you that while respecting another person's journey, I will not do it at the cost of my own self-respect and present needs. I request that you help me to remind myself that at times I am the one that most needs help, but that I do it in a way that is considerate to another's journey.

120 Sometimes it does not matter how balanced I feel when life does become difficult. It is not just a matter of partaking in Zen-like activities, that I know are not going to work in all instances. It is sometimes a matter of going with the anger and frustration, and riding the storm. A civilised public response is often called for in many situations, but in private and if warranted, all bets are off. I reckon there is a place for non-harming violence as a way of expressing my complete frustration at an uncontrollable situation. I pray to you for the strength and enlightenment to be able to ride these waves of frustration that occur in my life, that by using your life's example, I come to some acceptance.

121 Every day starts off the same. The sun rises in the East; when it heads below the Western horizon later in the day, these two events are the only things that can be guaranteed to have been the same as yesterday. I find this an awesome statistic, even more so as I get older. These days, when I open my eyes, I never take anything for granted. I might have a timetable of activities organised but I have and am still discovering, through experience, that life can be a whimsical entity when it comes to trying to have order in my day. In fact I sometimes think that life enjoys taking control away from me, at the time when I think that I most need it. I pray to you that, from the moment I open my eyes of a morning to when I close them of an evening, you help me to accept the path my life takes that day, even if it is one that I had not originally planned on taking. I also pray that I do this with a humorous attitude, doffing my hat to the whimsy of fate.

122 I look at the scenery and sometimes think that it never changes. I just have to look at images taken from generations past to know that this could not be further from the truth. The changes to the planet can be as slow as the movement of a glacier or as explosive as the constant bombardment from the ocean. I've even seen it change before my eyes, in the brutal quickness of a bush fire. Change is inevitable, whether it be the view in front of me; an activity that has just happened; the death of a loved one; or simply travelling a road I've never been on. Change is intimately connected with day to day living. One simple statement of truth is that I am not the same person today as the one who got out of bed yesterday morning. I pray for your help to always accept this basic truth, that I may be observant enough to pick up and learn from these changes in my life.

123 When I am exhausted and become irritated at a conversation or situation, I reckon that, in my case, the best course of action is to keep my mouth completely and firmly closed. Even if I think I am in the right I still consider it a sensible step. Why? Delivery of whatever I would like to say becomes extremely problematic when one is tired and just a tad cranky. This means I could cause the difficulty to escalate because I am also not thinking too straight and there is just the possibility that I am making an assumption. I pray to you that in these circumstances, you help me to gain the wisdom to know when to keep quiet and when to say what needs to be said; and that when I say it I say it with respect and understanding for the other person's situation.

September

Greenhill

124 When I look into a mirror, all I see is a reflection of myself. This reflection will only ever go skin deep. Then there is a different type of reflection, where I actually stand in front of another person and we mirror each other's personalities. If I do not like their personality, this can be an uncomfortable reality to tolerate. But I would also be downright stupid to ignore it. There is something to be learnt about myself in this situation, distasteful though I might find it. I pray to you that when I am faced with this type of mirror, you help me to accept that there is something in the other's personality that is reflected in me—a reflection that I need to look at, explore, own and not ignore.

125 It does not matter how articulate you are, or from what background, culture, etcetera you come from, you are sometimes going to do something that completely baffles a person not of your culture. Sometimes you can share a knee bending belly laugh. At other times, sadly, dreadful misunderstandings can occur. I pray to you to help humanity to see that our differences are a chance to learn about each other; that difference carries its own unique wisdom, and that we all take the time to find within ourselves that place of honour which helps us stretch out our hand in respect for another's journey, no matter how different it may be.

126 We say that we listen, but do we truly hear what the other person has to say? This morning, I was back-peddling from a bloke who barely had time to breathe, he was yakking so fast. What he was speaking about was probably important to him but I felt that it was inconsequential to me. But how did I know that if I wasn't hearing what he said? I pray to you that when I am faced with this situation again, I stop and take the time to hear what the person is saying. I will never see this person again but I apologise for not sharing some of my time with him.

127 Today is one of those special days where I am aiming to get a goal met. I am excited, as I did not think that I would get the opportunity. Sometimes dreams can be achieved with little fuss or preparation. At other times it can take a considerable amount of organisation, plus help from others. Today is one of those times where I need that help. The chances of me succeeding are pretty good, but there is always a But! I pray to you for your support in helping me to reach my goal. If that is not to be today, I know that I am going to be a little disappointed so please help me to accept that the journey is often the more important part in achieving my goals. I also thank you for the gift of friends and the encouragement that they give me.

128 There is nothing worse than someone trying to jolly you out of a disappointment, especially when that disappointment has just happened. We all have a right to experience it, and come to terms with what has happened. I pray to you that when I come across someone who is upset in this way, I don't try to jolly them but that I commiserate with their regret and not point out all the good things that might have happened on the way. Disappointment is sometimes not rational, but it is all too real. Help me to support others, whatever their truth, and allow me to wallow in my own for a while... but not for too long!

129 On the surface, absolutely nothing can beat the beauty of nature. Yesterday I travelled through many kilometres of wild flowers close to the road. I have never seen this type of beauty before. Millions of flowers of different species, each so unique. Each bend in the road brought its own awe-inspiring moment. And yet the quote: *'Beauty is in the eye of the beholder,'* seems quite apt here, as much of the colourful beauty was brought to you by what many would see as weeds. To many people, a weed is a waste of space; a noxious sprawl; financial difficulties. To me it is a plant outside of its natural environment. Through all of this I still see beauty. I pray to you that when I come across the so-called weeds in my life, I you help me to open my eyes to the lessons to be found in such scenery. I also pray that I am able to learn and discover how such beauty can occur. To me this speaks of amazing resilience. Even weeds have wisdom!

130 I reckon every single person on the face of the planet should be required to carry an image of their ancestors in their wallet/purse. I wonder if that would stop racism in its tracks. What ancestors you may ask? The ones from prehistoric times—Neanderthal man. He is the bloke that makes us all related. I pray to you that all of us show some courage to take a good hard look at ourselves and challenge any negative behaviour we have, in this or any area of human rights. I also pray that I assist humanity in their pursuit of personal freedom.

131 As children, there are three things that we looked forward to with great anticipation—Christmas, birthdays and holidays. I suppose I could add a fourth and say that going to town and getting some lollies was also something that had me jumping up and down with joy. As I have grown, I have often found that it is the anticipation of an event that brings me the joy. I do like to look forward to things, and do not like surprises so much. As we grow older, we often lose some of the punch that goes with that anticipatory joy. I pray to you that you help those of us who have lost this type of pleasure to find it again; that we look at the special days in our loved ones' life and find a way to spoil them a little. On our special days, let's help each other feel special.

132 One of the greatest gifts I have been given is to have a place that I call home. Not just a place to live, but a place where I feel comfortable and safe and where I can be myself. It is also a place where I can invite people in to enjoy each other's company. Home is a place where I can take time out and enjoy some alone time with myself. I am very lucky to have a home, not just a house. I pray to you that everyone is able to find a place that they can call home; where they feel safe and have the opportunity to rest and to be themselves.

133 Thanks and Sorry are, in my opinion, two of the most important words in my vocabulary. Without them, I can cause harm to anyone I communicate with. To me, it is most important to say Thanks when someone has given me something, either physically, or of their time. To not say Thanks would be wrong. The same goes with Sorry. If I have harmed someone, either knowingly or unknowingly, that person deserves my heartfelt apology. I pray to you that I continue to develop the skill of treating others as I would like to be treated; to do no harm wherever possible and to acknowledge the generosity of those around me.

134 This morning I dropped a rock and it broke into pieces. I picked it up and worked on getting it back together. It reminded me of our lives, and how we can be hurt and even broken with life's experiences. For all of us there is healing to some degree, but we can all be scarred by painful experiences. Some will never heal from their brokenness and the scarring will continue to fester throughout their life. I know not why this is so, but what I do know is that I can pray for all of us in our pain. I pray to you for those who are presently unable to come back from their brokenness; that one day the heaviness of their grief will be lightened by future happiness.

135 Early on in life I discovered that I should not make a promise that I could not keep. I found this out when others had made promises to me that they broke. Keeping my word is very important. To me it is about honour. I pray to you that before I make a promise to anyone, I make sure that it is not an impossible promise to keep; that if by some unforeseen circumstance I cannot do so, I apologise and find a way to lighten the other's disappointment.

136 It is without a doubt that I am not perfect. That I am a sinner is also beyond doubt. Sadly, I've also told a lie or two in my time… Alright, maybe more than one or two; I don't always tell the truth about my faults. But it brings me no comfort to know that no one else is perfect either, because my life is about my journey and no one else's. I pray to you to help me to challenge my behaviour, and help me to forgive myself for mistakes that I make and harm that I may cause.

137 Rarely do those with the loudest voice have anything to say that remotely resembles good sense, or that others wish to hear. I include myself in this judgement. I pray to you that when I wish to be heard, you help me to speak in a way that is perceptive, contains a modicum of sense and is spoken like a gentle breeze and not a scary storm.

138 My belief in myself and my abilities sometimes swings wildly into the negative. Sometimes it is outside influences that have me feeling poorly, and at other times I have no idea why I feel that I am not quite good enough. I pray to you that when I am feeling down, you help me to see all of the good things that I have done in my life, the achievements I have gained. Also help me to see that I am a good and worthy person; that I am loved and I am precious. Nobody can take that from me.

139 There are times in our lives when we look forward to an activity with anticipation of something good happening. For me it is a time to get away from the 'normalcy' of life; to have a quiet, peaceful and reflective time. I pray to you that when I have organised something, I find the sense to let go and let it happen. If it does not meet my expectations, that I stop being sorry for myself or the situation, and look at the lesson behind why it happened this way. I also pray for the strength to slow down and rest when it is needed. I'd reckon that sometimes this might be the lesson!

140 Every single one of us has faced the possibility of failure in our lives. For some that motivates them to try harder and for others it can leave them a quivering mess. I pray to you that we all see the possibility of failure as an opportunity to face our own personal demons; that we look deep within ourselves to find the strength to stand up and say: Yes, failure might be a possibility but it is not going to stop me from trying.

141 No matter their age, culture, religion, social standing or wealth, each person should be acknowledged on their special day—the day that they were born. On that day they brought uniqueness to the planet that has never been seen before. I pray that you help us generously acknowledge and honour all on their special day. I also pray that they have the strength to follow their true path, and work on accessing the potential that makes them unique.

142 How does one gauge their own personal success? Do you look within for the answer, or at the project results? I reckon that the best judge of my own success is me. I pray to you to help me to believe in myself and what I am able to accomplish; to turn away from negative comments, and to work on being positive in my comments to others.

143 There are times when I am scared of what my future may bring. Will I be able to pay my bills; will I get sick; will I lose loved ones? At times I feel that I am all alone and I have no one to support and care for me. It is a scary world we live in. I pray that when I feel like this, and even when I don't, I look to you for the comfort that I need to work through this fear. And when I need friendly support I ask for help. I have no problems in helping others in their need; why is it so difficult to ask for help with my own?

144 Have you ever had a belief that you strongly felt was the truth? And then someone comes along and challenges your truth with their viewpoint. What have you done about it? Did you dismiss their belief straight away; did you argue the facts; did you question their point of difference so that you could understand their belief better? In your heart of hearts did you believe that you were right and they were wrong? I pray to you that no matter what my beliefs and how another's belief is presented to me, I listen respectfully; that if I disagree with their viewpoint, I also discuss it courteously and keep an open mind. It is important to remember that we all have a right to a difference of opinion.

145 Have you ever reached the end of an activity or a holiday that you had been looking forward to and, depending on how well it went, you are either relieved or sad that you are heading back to 'normal' life? I pray to you that if I feel I need special moments in my life, then I request your aid in helping me to see and believe that there is always something special in my life. Help me to take time to explore, see and believe that the special in my life is me.

146 No matter how independent I think I might be, there is no way I can live life alone. My main goal in life is 'to know myself as fully as I am able'. I know that there is no way I will ever achieve this goal, as I will never fully know myself before I pass from this life. But it is the journey that is important, particularly relationships with friends and family. Without them, I would have little insight into myself. All the people I come across in life are my teachers. I pray to you that I pay attention to and respect all those who come across my path; that I listen to what they have to say. Furthermore, I need to remember that we are all life teachers to each other.

147 What right do I have to judge someone for their alleged wrong behaviour, especially when I also make mistakes? How many innocent people have been hit by stones thrown by the so-called righteous? These people need our prayers, not our condemnation. I pray to you that, guilty or innocent, it is not my place to judge. I pray for your strength and goodness to help me drop these stones of judgement, and pray for healing for those who have been hurt by malicious human behaviour.

148 Have you ever played a game where you try and memorise a number of objects, then they are hidden? The game is to try and remember as many of them as you can. From playing this game I realised that I do not have a perfect memory. Another one is when you have several people trying to describe an incident; you will almost always get several different answers. Our memory is not perfect, because we all see things differently. This is a great recipe for misunderstandings. I pray to you to help me remember this when my version of events do not coincide with another; that I realise that is what they truly believe. I need to accept that their version may be more accurate that what I saw. I also need to accept that I am not always right.

149 As I get older, my body finds it difficult to keep up with what I want to do. I see a hill that I want to climb, a beach I would love to walk on; games that I would like to play or social activities that I wish to attend. I cannot do most of these activities anymore and I sometimes feel as if life is beginning to pass me by. I pray to you that when I am feeling a little down like this, you help me see what I can still achieve; how I look at the rest of my life is about acceptance and attitude. I pray again that you help me accept the reality of my increasing disability and help me develop an optimistic attitude in facing my future.

150 One of the greatest joys in my life is working with and improving on the skills that I was born with. I pray that you help me develop my generosity of spirit and continue to learn that it is important that I do share these skills. I just never know what sharing may do to help another with their own abilities.

151 Have you ever looked at a tree and seen that some of the branches are dead? I see it as symbolic of myself and the often rough times that we all have in our lives. I sometimes feel like that tree; as if parts of me have died or that I have damaged an essential part of who I am. I pray to you that I spend time on reflecting on what has been damaged and, with your help, work on healing it.

152 It has been said so many times that it echoes around the planet: '*Dogs are a man's best friend*'. I only wish we could hear the corresponding echo: 'Flora and fauna and insects are humanity's best friend'. That way we might have a better chance of saving our planet. I pray to you that all of humanity begins to work on finding ways to help heal the damage that we have caused, and are continuing to cause, by our greed and excess. It may be an obvious phrase but this is the only home we have; we desperately need to open our eyes to the truth and work on this together.

153 Yesterday I was able to achieve all of the goals I set for myself, plus a bit more. I was so grateful. I thank you for helping this to occur. Some might ask why I am thanking Mother Mary when I did all the work. My reply is that this is the path of my Faith. I believe in the Powers greater than myself, and that they help me to achieve what I set out to do. I pray to you that I always feel you in my life, and that my Faith will continue to strengthen me as I walk my journey; that those who follow the path of Faith might be an example to those who struggle with their belief.

October

Out my back door

154 Creation is not done in isolation. First you begin with a need, then comes an idea. Many, many years ago someone remembered that the wind on their face cooled them down. Thus began humanities journey with the preservation of food. The road for those who are inventors is one that is often filled with dead-ends. But what I admire about these inquisitive minds is that they never stop trying. Without these amazing people we would have not invented refrigeration, nor made it off the planet. Even though most of us might not be able to make a rocket that would fly us to the moon, we all have resourceful minds that help us to solve problems. I pray to you that we use our minds to help us with our own needs, the needs

of our neighbours, the needs of all of those who live on this planet and the planet itself. I also pray that we all find the strength of character to address these needs.

155 We all dramatise incidents in our lives. How often have we heard the statement that this or that or, even, our lives have been ruined because of a minor incident that went wrong? Yes, our lives may have been affected, often for only a short while, but how can we say that our lives have been ruined? I pray to you that you help us all to look at the things that have gone wrong in our lives in a different light; to see them as an opportunity, not a disaster. Yes, it might seem disastrous at the moment but, with an attitudinal change, a so-called disaster could easily become a positive in our lives.

156 One of the goals I have while walking this planet is to know myself as fully as I am able. That is going to be a lifelong endeavour, as I believe that I will never fully know myself. I observe others as they make their journey through life. I admire the courage that they show as they step outside their comfort zones to challenge and discover new things about who they are. I pray that you help me find that same courage to continue on my own path of self-discovery; and that you help to gently challenge us all to explore our potential and assist it in becoming a reality.

157 The one thing that I appreciate in learning about myself is that when I discover something new, it fills in part of the jigsaw of who I am. It also gives me direction on which way to head in my never-ending quest for self-knowledge. It is a bit like searching for treasure, because each little bit I learn is precious to me. I pray to you that no matter how tough life gets, I will always find the time to be with myself, sifting the wheat from the chaff of daily life, looking for the next piece in the jigsaw. I thank you for the gift of myself and the skills to journey this road in self-discovery.

158 We all live with fear in our lives, from fear of the unknown, the future, illness, finances … the list is endless. Some of us live with many fears and at times it stops us living. I pray to you that when

I am faced with my own personal fear, I find the courage to stand up to it; that I use that fear as a tool to help me move forward in my life, not to stall in the one spot. For to overcome my fear is to find the joy in living.

159 When someone says 'No' to me, what do I immediately think? The truthful answer is that my response or reaction is a good indication of how I am presently emotionally balanced; in other words, how I feel about myself. Do I assume that they don't like me, or do I thank them and go and find someone else to help me with my present need? The truth is that we all make assumptions. Sometimes they are even right! I pray to you that you help me to take people at face value; that when they say No, they do it for their own needs and no other reason.

160 Never underestimate the power of a simple thanks. How often have you done something for another and the other person never thanked you in any way? It can hurt. And then another person will go above and beyond and will even give you a little gift with the thanks. I know that receiving thanks makes me feel good. I pray to you that we all look at ourselves when it comes to thanking others; that we make an effort to be generous in our thanks. A simple thank you can make my day. Let us all work to help make each other's day.

161 No matter whom you work for or what you do, when you have the power to affect someone's life by the decisions you make or the information that you have to give, either positively or negatively, it should be done with grace and consideration. I pray to you that if I am ever placed in this position, I treat people the way I would like to be treated … efficiently, compassionately and with the utmost respect.

162 One of the greatest joys in life is to be given the unconditional love of a child. To me, that love is like being bathed in sunlight. When I am with a child that loves me, I sometimes think it is like being in the presence of the Divine as it can feel so pure. I pray to you that I continue to learn that my love is a gift to share, and that it is not a commodity to barter.

163 When I've been hurt by someone I sometimes wish to strike out and hurt them back. It has been said that, '*To err is human and to forgive, divine.*'* Well, it is times like this when I definitely know that I am human. I pray to you that before I even think of striking out in my pain, I take time to consider what it may mean to me and how I would feel if I harmed another human being. I've always said that I wish others to treat me the way I would like to be treated, so how can I do any less for others? Even if I feel that the other is in the wrong, help me to forgive and to move on.

* Originally from a poem written in 1711 by English poet Alexander Pope titled: *An Essay on Criticism, Part II.*

164 When I was a kid I can remember my mum saying that events would 'happen at the right time'. This was usually after something was postponed, or one of us kids forgot to do something. This saying puzzled me because I could not understand why there would be a right time for something to happen. I think what mum was trying to teach me was that it was not the end of the world if something doesn't happen at the time it was organised, and basically not to stress about it. I pray that I learn that there are times when I need to let things go, because something more important came up. I also pray that I will continue to learn wisdom from wherever I find it, and that I don't get frustrated with things not happening when I want them to. As my mum would say: 'It will happen at the right time for me.'

165 When I am feeling jealous I reckon it is because I am not accepting my lot in life. To me, yearning after another person's possessions or lifestyle is just plain wrong. It is also a denial of my own true path of self-discovery, that I have been walking these many years. I pray to you that when I am doing it hard and things are looking a little greener on the other side of the fence, I look at my own life and where I have come from. I would reckon that there are a lot of experiences in my life that I could stand up and be proud of. The only good I can see in jealousy is the opportunity for me to reflect on why I am jealous and what I am jealous about. This could be a chance to learn a little bit more about me.

166 Motivation or lack of it will cause difficulty in any project that I am wishing to complete. The bigger or tougher the project, the more motivation I need. For example, I find it very difficult to motivate myself these days to do anything physical. I know this is not impossible when the motivation is right, like seeing a top shot that has me reaching for my camera. I pray to you for your help in remembering that there is one thing I should reflect on when working on a project, and that is the journey itself. This is where I learn the most. I have also discovered that, at times, the outcome may not be what I envisioned it to be.

167 Nobody can be on top of their game 100% of the time. At many points in our lives we are going to have to ask for help. It can be a humbling experience, especially when we dislike asking for help. I pray to you that I find the strength to accept that I am not an island; that I reach out when I am in need; and that I stretch out my hand when I see someone else in need.

168 One of the greatest joys in life is to sit and watch children play. It is a pleasure to watch the fun that they are having. Their use of their imagination is a gift that should be encouraged every chance we get. It is their imagination that is going to help them walk the path to their adult selves, for from imagination comes our dreams. I pray to you that if I feel I have lost my imagination, you help me take the time to listen to the children, and sit and play with them. They will gladly teach me how to play again. We all have the gift of imagination … a gift that can be re-energised by the voice of a child, and from the child within ourselves.

169 If I had to draw a picture of myself and my life, I would draw something that looked like a road map. There would be one major road, with many sealed and unsealed roads taking off in all directions from the main road. Some would be dead-ends meaning I would have to back track to find another path. Some would go on for ages travelling through places I've never been before and eventually meeting back up with the main road. Other roads would have me travelling away from the noise and bustle of my 'ordinary' life, so that I could find time with myself in quiet reflection. There are times when I travel my main road and am brought to a sudden stop, as the road is damaged and cannot be travelled until repaired. Sometimes I take a detour to get around the damage. But there is going to be a time when that old damage is going to cause problems on the road ahead. The potholes that arise cannot always be avoided, but have to be repaired before I can continue on. The further I travel on my life's journey, the more I grow and change. Who I am and who I become is a product of my choices and experiences. But I believe that it is my Soul and my Faith that are my compass on my journey. I pray to you to give me the strength to never leave that compass behind; that I always ask for your advice when I reach a crossroads in my life, and don't ever forget to say thank you. And when it is time to have fun I ask you to have fun with me.

170 When I look at someone I do not particularly like I think of two things—one it is not a very Christian thought even though reality tells me that we all know people in our lives that we don't like. The other thought is the question—Why don't I like them? In my much less mature days, I would not have anything to do with them. Problem solved! These days I have the belief that they are in my life for a reason, and it is in my best interest to find out why. Over the years I have discovered that when I think about what I don't like in that person, it is usually what I am not keen on in myself. I pray to you that I gain the strength to be more than just polite to those I do not like; that I do not ignore them. They have come into my life to teach me something. I should treat them the way that I would like to be treated, with dignity and respect.

171 When the sun comes up, the morning light shines softly on the land. Depending on cloud cover and the angle of the sun during the day, I can often see different things within the same view. To me it speaks of possibilities. I pray to you that when I first see the morning light, I see these possibilities in my day and that the changing light shows me more as the day progresses. And at the end of each day I am thankful for what I have learned and achieved. In reality I know that not every day I live is going to be positive. So, I also pray that on those hard days, I look for the good in them. I know there will be something to find … there can be a gentle joy to be discovered in any day where grief and pain is found.

172 I have been sitting and watching the same view for the last twenty years. I have become accustomed to it but I will never get sick of it. It shows me a different face nearly every day. We all have different faces and we express ourselves in different ways at different times, and for different reasons. And we all have a different Faith. Many of us might belong to one of the many recognised religions, but it is my belief that every single one of us travels a different path of Faith. How can we not as we are all so unique? I pray to you that we all show respect for each other's Faith path; and that instead of condemning or misunderstanding another's Faith, we take time to communicate with them to discover our differences. We might just find that we are not so different after all. I also pray that if we believe that we have the right to practice our Faith without fear, then we need to ask ourselves: Doesn't everyone else deserve the same right?

173 Every new day is like a blank canvas. I wonder what I am going to have achieved by the time I go to sleep that night. What I do hope and I pray to you for is that I will make a difference in my life. I also pray that when I am with another, I can encourage them in a positive way; and that at the beginning of each day we all feel strong enough to be there for each other.

174 We wouldn't be human if we did not make mistakes. Mostly they are small but some of them can be real doozies. I'd even term some of my mistakes as 'dumb,' because I cannot believe that I did something so stupid. I wonder what a smart mistake would look like! I suppose it would be the valuable lesson I learnt from the consequences of that mistake. I pray to you that I accept the fact that I am going to make more mistakes in the future; that I take time to learn from them and, if I harm another by mistake, that I seek forgiveness.

175 The more focused I am on an issue, the less likely I am to stuff-up; the more clarity I can gain, the better able I am to achieve what I am aiming for. For me, focus is also important when it comes to prayer and meditation. I pray to you that during the times when it is important for me to focus, I am able to concentrate and live in the moment totally attentive on what is important now.

176 I know that over the years, even though it is well meaning, some advice has driven me to distraction and some very un-Christian thoughts. I pray to you that I find the strength in the future not to give advice unless it is asked for, and that if/when I am offered advice, I accept it with grace and in the manner it was given.

177 I have always said that I will never be perfect, but I will never stop trying to achieve perfection. I also believe that good enough will never be good enough. I pray to you that in my dealings with others or in working on my goals, I will always give the best of me and be the best that I can.

178 One of the things I do not like about myself is my ability to tell a lie. And I am not talking about my creative talent to spin a good yarn. I've been known to tell a lie to protect myself or someone else, but what I don't like about some of my lies is my lack of courage in telling the truth. I pray to you for help in challenging myself when I know am about to lie; to ask myself the question—who is it going to harm if I tell the truth? And also ask myself: If it feels wrong when I do it, why am I not listening to myself?

179 When things start to go wrong in my day, I used to and still do, at times, get really irritated. Yesterday I got a flat battery and, for once, I did not get frustrated. I immediately started to look for the positives in the situation. Instead of it being a frustratingly negative experience, I ended up having a lovely morning. I pray to you that in the future, when things start to go wrong, I use this experience as an example of turning the negative into a positive; that I challenge my attitude; and continue to learn from each experience.

180 Arrogance is not a trait that looks good on me. If used poorly it can be demeaning to others and even to myself. Every single one of us has a skill that we are better at than others. So, to my mind arrogance is misplaced. I pray to you that we all challenge our behaviour when it comes to our pride; that we acknowledge our successes with humility; and that we respectfully show how proud we are in what we or our loved ones achieve.

181 I looked out the window this morning and I saw a partial rainbow. It brought a smile to my face. I know that a rainbow is simply light refracted through raindrops, but for me the beauty of it is a symbol of hope and optimism in life. I pray to you that, like the rainbow, we all take the time to stop and look at the beauty that is all around us; that beauty might not be cloaked like a rainbow but it is there if only we would take the time to look.

182 I know that I still have a lot of work to do when it comes to judging others. One of those lessons is that, in the past, I have made the mistake of basing my opinion of someone on what another tells me. I need to remember that we all see things differently. I pray to you that in the future, if I draw an opinion on someone, I make it through my own observations and not someone else's; that I don't make a judgement based on just one contact; and never ever judge a person just by what I see.

183 Change is an integral part of our lives. For each step we take, yesterday is further away and tomorrow is that much closer. There is change in each one of those steps. Most steps are relatively easy, but there are some that take courage. Some challenge us to step into the unknown, and to walk places we've never been before. I pray to you that when I am faced with difficult changes in my life, you help me step outside my comfort zone and face the challenge of doing something that I have never done before.

184 Have you ever found yourself grumbling and muttering a few not so polite words at the lack of courtesy of people on the roads? I reckon that I am a polite road user. Why then can't others show a little bit of respect? Well, that was a rather self-righteous attitude! I pray to you that we all honestly challenge the appropriateness of our own behaviour, whether it is on the road or in other parts of our life. I am not as perfect as my traffic tickets would indicate!

November

Old Catholic Church, Sherwood

185 When I make a promise to someone I feel honour bound to keep it. I have given my word, and my word is a very precious thing to me. When I have kept that promise, I feel as if I have achieved something honourable; it is important to me. It is a part of who I am. I pray to you that in the future, I think seriously before I make a promise. If I don't think I can keep a promise, I shouldn't make it. The challenge in life, and I also pray for help with this, is to be the best that I can and to discover what my best can be.

186 Do you consider yourself superstitious? Well then, have you ever said those most famous words—'It can't get any worse than this?' Well it did for me, yesterday, and living just got that little bit harder. I want to pray for healing and have it happen instantaneously, but I feel as if that would be presumptuous. So instead I pray to you that I will accept this setback graciously; that I do not become an island; and that I swallow my pride and ask for help.

187 I might look at another person's problems or pain and think that mine are so much worse. But there is no way on this earth that I can make that kind of comparison. They have to live through their pain and problems. I don't. I pray to you that when looking at another's pain, I don't compare; that I be compassionate and acknowledge that we all do it tough at times.

188 I was given a gift beyond price yesterday. A friend overcame her pain and fear to help get me to where I needed to go. I was totally amazed when I found out but in my brokenness, I said to her that she should not have done it. In a sense, I was trying to negate her sacrifice. And her sacrifice is what she gifted me with. I pray to you that in future, when someone helps me, I honour and accept their choice. My friend has amazing compassion. She is a gift, not just to me, but to all she comes in contact with. She is a teacher and an example. I thank you that she has crossed my path.

189 I sit here, wordless, feeling somewhat distressed. I had a need that was not met. I pray to you that in the future, I take a deep breath and am gracious with the people that I am dealing with. Sometimes I have to accept that the person/people who are supposed to have the answers do not. So I need to take a deep breath, accept this reality and try to find the answer somewhere else.

190 Some of my best photos are the ones that are in my mind. That is because I either did not have my camera, or I was not prepared. Some of my best images are because I was prepared, or I was lucky, and was at the right place and time. But being prepared is not going to guarantee success every time. I pray to you that I always take the time to consider how I am going to attempt future projects; that I don't always charge in with a '*She'll be right,*' attitude. There are times when I will need to look at each step I take, to give myself the best opportunity of success.

191 Have you ever been in a situation where you said to yourself: 'That was great, but it could have been better?' How many 'if only' moments have we all had, when we think something is not quite good enough? I pray to you that I take the time to accept life as it is; to continue to acknowledge that life is not just about getting what I want but challenging myself to do the best that I can, and congratulating others on the best that they have done.

192 I've been known to do one or two stupid things in my life. In fact, my mother blames all of her grey hairs on me. I won't deny that I was really good at finding trouble. I would say, though, that I have become more deliberate as I've reached the adult part of this amazing life journey. I pray to you that we all give our young ones the opportunity to get out in life and get dirty; to come home with amazing stories of the day; and to listen to those stories as if that was the most important thing in the world. Whether we know it or not, one of our jobs in life is to help all of the children play, including the child within.

193 Acceptance of my history is part of the fertiliser that I need for my personal growth. If I do not accept where I have come from, how can I even begin to plan my future path? I pray to you for assistance in working through the story that is me to help me find and accept those parts of my history that I have difficulty with; to gain understanding into why I find it so difficult; and to realise that my history is what makes me who I am today.

194 I look out into the garden and, instead of looking at things I can no longer do, I look at the projects that I achieved when I could. I pray to you that I continue to look for ways to gain acceptance of my present path; instead of focusing on what I cannot do any more, to look at what I have achieved since I was injured and what I continue to achieve to the present day. We all have our crosses to bear. Our job is to find a way to carry it as comfortably as we can.

195 Excuses! We've all used them. 'But I'm telling the truth,' I've heard myself cry in the past. The only good thing about an excuse is if they are creatively entertaining. I pray to you for your help, that instead of making excuses I find ways to finish what I am working on; if I cannot find a way, I ask for help. And, I repeat, that I am not an island!

196 Have you ever found yourself doing something for no rhyme or reason … the activity just does not make sense? Mine is counting the horses every morning that I can see out my back window. I explain it away as a centring exercise. But for whatever bizarre reason it brings me comfort. I pray to you that I consider the activities that I do which appear to make no sense. One day in the future, the reason may become clearer. Life is not just about the serious and work-related activities. Like many questions, there is often no answer and for some activities there may be no known reason.

197 Yeats wrote: '*Strangers are friends that I have not met yet.*' I live with this attitude, and I reckon that the chances of it coming true are pretty good. One of my aims in life is to continue meeting new friends. I pray to you that I continue treating with grace and respect the friends that I do have, and that I have a welcoming attitude to those who are presently strangers.

198 Whinging seems to be a sport in some cultures. To my chagrin, I have at times made an art of the creative complaint. What do I achieve by telling others how bad my night was, or how much pain I am in? I pray to you that I continue to work humorously on finding the answer to how I am feeling. Yes, I know that I am miserable at times, but I would much rather be entertaining while getting my misery off my rather ample chest. I consider humour a cleansing way of achieving this.

199 Focusing too much on the down times can be such a waste of the happy times. I pray to you for help to walk into the happy and calm times when I am feeling down; that I forgive others for the harm that they may have unintentionally caused me and vice versa. It is important that I have a good balance of happy in my life, as I won't ever get the chance to live that part of my life again.

200 I counted fourteen flowering bushes in my garden this morning. What was amazing was that each flower on each individual bush was different from every other flower on the bush. I see the planet Earth as not only my home but I also see it as my teacher. I pray to you that I open my eyes to the lessons that can be found all around me. I also pray that we all have the opportunity to nurture our potential, so that we can indeed share our unique beauty with others and this planet that we call home.

201 I do not like it that I have been injured. I do not like it that my mobility is deteriorating. I do not like it that I can no longer do certain things. I might not like these and other situations as they sometimes make me as cranky as a cut snake, but I mostly do accept my reality. I pray to you that when I am feeling cranky and low, I take time to look at the positive in my life; at the paths that have opened up because of these changes in my life; and that I also continue to pray for that acceptance of my reality.

202 A friend once said to me that they thought they were doing it tough, until they saw someone else who was doing it tougher. She went on to quote the aphorism—*'I thought I had it tough because I had no shoes and then I saw someone without any feet.'* I truly believe that we cannot compare our journey with another's. We can only live and experience our own journey. I pray to you that we respect our own path and the path of others; that we acknowledge that our own pain and life experiences are no worse or easier than another's. It is just different.

203 I sit here on this beautiful clear morning waiting for inspiration … waiting! It is not as if there is not a lot to pray about. I have a lot to be thankful for and there are a lot of people who are in need of your compassionate hand, including myself at times. So, I pray to you for all of those who are in need of your help; that we all look for inspiration to help ourselves and that we acknowledge that, though we might not have the words, we can still pray.

204 I look at a young bird flying and it reminds me of the joy I felt the first time I succeeded at something. I don't think it would take any imagination to know how someone feels when they are unsuccessful at a particular project. But the truth is we cannot be effective at everything we do. I pray to you that we all accept our reality when it comes to achievement. I also pray that if I do not accomplish my desired outcome, I am gracious to those who do.

205 I once thought that praying was for a time when I was in trouble. I'd rarely think of saying a prayer of thanks for when things went right. As a woman of Faith, I now believe that you, Mother Mary, give me strength to achieve success and help me through the tough times. So, today I pray to you for greater strength in my Faith; that you help me to remember to pray a prayer of thanks just for being alive; and a prayer for those who are doing it tough.

206 There are times when I come across people who are disrespectful of others. To return that disrespect would be neither the smart nor the Christian thing to do. But I do know that to bring myself to that level is to disrespect myself. I pray to you for your help in finding the strength and wisdom to be respectful of all, no matter what. When I leave this planet I would like to be able to say to myself that I am proud of my behaviour and the paths that I have walked.

207 One of the greatest kindnesses a person can give is to overcome their own discomfort and fear to help out another person who is in need. I pray to you that I learn from the example that they teach with their lives; and that I can overcome my own discomfort to help others.

208 Yesterday I ran into some old work colleagues. One of them said to me that I had not changed a bit. It bemused me somewhat because I know that I have changed. I pray to you that we acknowledge that we all change over the years. That is not always apparent, nor is the depth of a person's character. I also pray that we are respectful of each other's path.

209 We all believe that we are a failure at some point in our lives. Just because we are not successful in one activity, does not mean that we as a person are a total failure. I pray to you that when I do feel like this, I take the time to focus on those activities in my life when I have been successful. Sometimes we do not have the skills to be a success in certain activities, but this does not mean that I am a failure. I have just learnt that there are some things I cannot do. Learning something about myself that I cannot do can be frustrating, but it is never a failure!

210 Part of human nature is in our ability to make choices. Sometimes choices are taken away through uncontrollable circumstances, like an injury. But we don't give up making choices because of it. We start making different ones. I pray to you that, when I feel that control of my life has been taken from me, please remind me that I never fully had control in the first place. Although life circumstances can take some choices from me, I can still guide myself onto paths that will help me achieve my goals. Sometimes I might have to let some goals go, and make new ones. I also pray that you help me to accept that my life is not always easy, but that it continues to have meaning.

211 How many of us lived our lives with monikers given to us by our family and friends ... Ace, Shorty, Bluey, Hot Shot, Peanut, Slim and other kinds of cute nicknames? Then there are ones like Black Sheep and Biggest Disappointment. There are also many nasty and inappropriate ones out there. How many of us try to live up to some of the names that we have been given? How many of us were hurt by them? I pray to you that I realise the damage a nickname can cause, even if I think I am being funny. I pray that when I am playful with someone, I think very carefully and am respectful with my games.

212 Sometimes when I am hurting I want to lash out at others. I can get so frustrated that I lose my cool. I pray to you that when I am in pain and hurting, you help me to step back from others. If I cannot do this, help me to find the courage to explain how I am feeling. It might help to be honest in explaining where I am at.

213 I know that humour can be a great tool in defusing a tense situation, or when we are feeling stressed; or maybe just to bring a smile to another's face. One thing I learnt very early is never to use it at the expense of another. Any time I use humour, I need to remember that it can fall flat and cause harm. I pray to you that we all learn how to use humour wisely; that we do not use it to make fun of another; and that when we use it we do it to lighten life and bring a smile to the face of others.

214 We've all been known to wear masks for various reasons. Often it is to protect ourselves in some way; sometimes we do not want others to see our pain, our fear. With a mask we can feel personally stronger and safer. I myself have perfected the mask of the clown, because I did not want people to know I sometimes did not feel good enough. I pray to you that I continue to work to take off my masks as often as I can, so that people can see who I truly am.

December

Macleay Valley Way, Clybucca

215 It has been said that 'only the good die young!' I'd like to say that aging is a badge of honour. How so? Aging is a road where we experience and collect much knowledge. The older we live, the more family and friends we lose and the more changes there are in the world and ourselves. Some people live to the point where they are the last person in their generation. From my place on my life's journey, I have great admiration and some sadness for these people.

I pray to you that we all take the time to honour the older members of our community; that we continue to acknowledge their participation in the past and present growth of our community. That we reflect on the loss of friends and family, and acknowledge the loneliness that the aging members of our family and community may feel.

216 There are changes happening every day in my life. Sometimes the changes are made by me. Sometimes they are made by others, but affect my life profoundly. Even though something may affect me, I do not always have the ability to stop it. We rarely think about how the choices we make can affect others. I pray to you that, even if I think a choice is a totally personal one, and only mine to make, I take the time to reflect on it and consider the possible consequences it may have on others. While it is my right to make choices for myself, about myself, I do not have the right to adversely affect others because of it.

217 Have you ever found yourself looking at another person and thinking that you are better than them? I was raised in a racist town, where I was taught through example that white skin was better than black. To my own distress, and from one who considers herself a good person, I never questioned this until I left town. I have never knowingly done anything racist but at times, to my chagrin, I have found my thought patterns to be racist. I pray to you that I continue to challenge those thought patterns; that I support First Nations activities in the community; and that I, who considers herself Christian, continually question my behaviour and thoughts towards those who are considered 'different.'

218 I've always wondered why Christmas seems to be the only season for giving. To me, it also seems to be the season for family fights, or over-indulgence in both food and gifts. While many work really hard on reviving the spirit of Christmas, I personally would like to see the end of the commercialisation of this period. I would also appreciate it if someone found a way to hide all the canned Christmas carols! I pray to you that we all rediscover in our hearts the joy and spirit of Christmas, and that we don't just bring it out during the festive season, but carry that joy and spirit all year round.

219 I once saw a mosquito flying through the rain. I thought that feat was something of a miracle. I believe there are many everyday miracles happening in the world today. To me a miracle can be as simple as seeing a need in another, and then stretching out my hand and helping them to get that need met. Miracles can be as gentle as a breeze in giving that helping hand. I pray to you that we allow ourselves to become the instrument of that everyday miracle; that we take time to look and see the needs that are around us; and to help to bring others into the light of their own potential. To me this is truly a miracle!

220 I often hear on the news people talking about those who have died in tragic circumstances. They say lovely things about them. It got me wondering how often we said these same things to these people when they were alive. I pray to you that we all take the time to praise others. It is important that they know that we can see the good in them. I don't believe that we do this enough, especially to those special people in our lives. I also pray that I tell them often that I love them.

221 Rain is the life-giving blood of the planet. Not enough can be disastrous and too much can also be devastating. Without rain, all life would cease to exist. Nothing would grow. And like anything, the earth and everything upon it needs balance. Yet humanity is disturbing that balance by the terrible activities we continue to pursue in the name of advancement, which many also see as greed. I pray to you that we all challenge our own footprint upon this earth, and that we question ourselves—do we really need what we are consuming? Look at what we are throwing away—ask ourselves: Can we or another reuse it? I also pray that all of humanity develops respect towards our planet; to help heal the damage to the only home that we have.

222 Last evening, two birds shattered my peaceful reflection of the day by flying into the window that I was sitting near. It was somewhat of a shock. I love this spot for its very peacefulness. Whilst the birds, the window and I survived, it left me reflecting on the experience. What came to my mind was the thought that I should never take anything for granted. So, I pray to you that I continually reflect on the things that I may take for granted: my quality of life; my home, my family & friends; my health, my freedom; that I don't just accept that I have the right to them, but that I am thankful for them and the chances I have been given in life. I also pray that I continually work on improving, not just my physical circumstances, but my spiritual ones as well; and for the wellbeing of my neighbours.

223 Many years ago, I discovered that we all suffer emotional pain. As I grew into adulthood, I began to understand more deeply the fragility of the human ego, and how an unthinking word can play a part in damaging that ego. I pray to you that in the future, you help me to deliberate on my words before they are said; that instead of words of condemnation, I speak words of kindness and truth; for a well-spoken word can begin to mend another's ego, which can then help them see the goodness within themselves.

224 My past has helped to make me who I am today. And my memories of my past are an internal library of my journey through my life. At times, they are easy to access and at others, I have to work real hard to bring them to the surface. Sadly, some I have forgotten forever, or are so fragmented that they are confusing. I am not only part of my own memories, I am also a part of the memories of all I have come into contact with. I pray to you that when dealing with others, I help to make their memories positive ones; that they find happiness in their memories; and that the memories help them discover more about themselves.

225 As I have lived my life, I have had to face many challenges. I can remember, after one particular incident, my mother saying to me that these challenges in life are good for my character. Me, well I wasn't so sure. How wrong I discovered myself to be, when I began to learn things about myself during these times. I pray to you that, before I face future challenges, I look for ways to emotionally support myself, so that I do not do it alone; that I ask for help, if and when I need it. And yes, I have been praying this prayer a lot, as all through my life I have had difficulties in asking for help.

226 I have found, over the years, that making excuses for my actions is demeaning to myself and disrespectful to those I make the excuses too. Of what possible benefit can it be to accept a fleeting comfort, which turns quickly to disquiet when I realise that basically I told a lie. I pray to you that I find the courage and strength to stand up for my actions, even if I think that might put me in a bad light. My word is important to me. I also pray that I am always respectful to my own truth.

227 How often at the end of telling a story have you heard someone say: 'That is unbelievable!'? Often it is because the story is so way out, we don't believe what the person said. We've all been known to embellish stories in the name of humour. And every single one of us will give a contradictory report after having seen the same incident. That is because we all see things differently. I pray to you that we all learn to trust each other, and respect each other's version of events. Just because we did not see it does not make it an untruth. I also pray that I continue to learn to have faith in others.

228 For me, celebrating is a joyful activity used to uplift, acknowledge and acclaim certain feats accomplished by individuals, cultures, countries, religions etc. To me, it is important to celebrate those moments when we exceed normal life activities. I pray to you that we all take the time to celebrate with our friends, family and community those times when we do go above and beyond; and that we do it in a respectful and acceptable manner.

229 In my opinion one of our greatest challenges is not just in the acceptance of approaching death, but in living it while we are preparing for dying. We all react differently to the news of our impending doom. Some people take to their beds, while some set goals to challenge themselves in ways they have not challenged themselves before. I pray to you that, as I move closer to my final days on this planet, I continue to work on the goals that I have set and to add more goals to my 'kark-it' list. My final goal in life is to leave this planet with goals half completed, and a list of goals that could fill another lifetime.

230   As I was growing up, I gave various reasons as to why I had lied to someone. Usually it was because I was trying to protect myself. I pray to you that I continue to learn that when I lie, the person that I hurt the most is me; that I also continue to realise that it is wrong to lie. My word depends on the truth, and if I cannot trust my own word … well then what can I trust!

231   One of my definitions of family is as a platform from where, as a young one, I was able to launch myself as an individual. My family was, and still is, a support to help me in my explorations about the world I live in, the people that inhabit this world and myself. I pray to you that I continue to acknowledge my family, as well as the strength and courage I have gained to take the paths that I have. As I have reached adulthood, I have realised that the support mechanisms I have developed through the years will not break, but continue to change to meet my future needs.

232   I always knew that I lived in 'The Lucky Country.' But it was not until the planet was hit by Covid that I realised how truly lucky most Australians were. Why most? We still have many poor Australians living in all parts of this continent. If I was to ask them, would they say that they lived in a Lucky Country? I am sure all of those suffering from all types of abuse: the homeless; the spiritually & financially poor; those who do not have access to good health care; the culturally isolated etc., would not agree. I pray that I look deeply at the culture of the community that I live in, and challenge myself to judge the support I give to it; ask myself can I do better, and can I help others to do better? That I take time to support our community leaders—those who have the strength and foresight to see a need and then to work on getting it met. I also pray that every time I think of this country as the lucky country, I think of and pray for those Australians who are not so lucky.

233   Have you ever procrastinated when something needed to be done? I can answer this one in the affirmative many times, especially when it is about asking someone for a favour or help for me. Why is that so? Am I afraid that they will say 'no,' or do I think that I am not worth having a favour done for me? Once upon a time I might have said 'yes' to both of these questions, but not anymore. I know that I am a good person and worthy of help. I pray to you that, when others asked me for help, I think of the times when I did not feel so worthy. If at this time I have to say 'no,' help me to help them understand that it is for my reasons. Also before I say 'no,' I should remember the times when someone has gone out of their way to help me. Sometimes it is important to say 'no,' but I need to remember how it felt when someone said 'yes' to me.

234 There are times in my life when I have felt powerless, especially with the issues I am presently living with. I sometimes wonder what meaning my life can possibly have. There have been times when there has been absolutely no quality of life, or enjoyment in living. Nor can I give my life meaning by comparing it to the journey of another who is also doing it tough. I pray to you that, during these times when I am feeling powerless, I spend time in prayer; that I find the courage to allow myself to live in acceptance of my journey; that I work on learning about who I am and, most importantly, that I remember how to laugh.

235 I think it is somewhat ironical that I grew up believing I was not good enough, for I grew up in a town that had a lot of racism; a town where I was taught that white was better than black. Talk about mixed messages! Two things I have learnt from my journey are that I am good enough, and that I am also no better than anyone else. I pray to you that we all learn not to send mixed messages; that we learn and demonstrate that we are all equal; that instead of withdrawing from someone from another culture or belief system, we learn about their differences. To others from another culture, our beliefs can be just as confusing. Understanding and valuing another's culture and beliefs is not about disrespecting our own, it is about learning to live in harmony with each other.

236 I am reminded almost daily of my imperfect nature. I did something wrong recently. I did it without thought. I cannot justify my action. My soul feels the pain of my wrongdoing. I pray to you that I accept and acknowledge when I have done wrong; that I take time to question my future actions; that I seek forgiveness and apologise appropriately, and remind myself that wallowing can be just as wrong for the soul.

237 It is my belief that, when we are born, we are all given the potential to achieve certain skills. Many of us go on to achieve what we set out to do. Just a few of us go on to achieve fame in our area of expertise. It is also my belief that no one is given potential fully formed. We have to find the determination to achieve and we have to work at it every day. I pray to you that we find the motivation to work at the potential we have been given; that we don't give up when it becomes hard. And to remember that achievement does not have to be worked at alone.

238 When I am feeling down and doing it tough, I find it difficult to trust in my own abilities or even to believe in myself. I pray to you that, during the down times, I find the strength to trust in myself again; that I always take time to pray and meditate each day; and that I continue to look at and applaud myself for that which I have achieved in my life. To put it simply, life is not easy. Smile and deal with it.

239 If we think that Christmas is only for children, then we've lost the spirit of Christmas. For me, it is not about eating ourselves silly, or going into debt buying gifts for our loved ones. To me, Christmas is about the birth of Hope, through Love and Faith. Each year is a reminder to me of that Hope. I pray to you to help me live the spirit of Christmas in my heart; to remind myself that I do not have to become involved in the commercialism of Christmas; and that I live by example my meaning of Christmas.

240 I had a conversation with a friend recently. We are both Catholic and we talked about our Faith. As we talked, I sat there thinking to myself that some of his beliefs were a little way out there, but what impressed me the most was his deep conviction in his Faith. I pray to you that I am continually reminded that each individual's path of Faith is different and unique—not just within Catholicism, but all Faiths within the world; and I pray that we respect each other's journey. I also pray that we support the freedom of all people to express their Faith.

241 It is difficult at times to know when I have reached my limits … or maybe it's that I have just run out of motivation. Yesterday the question arose for me—how hard do I push myself? I was halfway through an activity when I realised that I had pushed too hard. It was very frustrating, as I was motivated but I just did not have the energy. I pray to you that I learn to accept my limitations; that I realise there are times when motivation is not enough; and that at these times I need to swallow my pride and ask for help.

242 There have been times in my life when I wished that I could get rid of some of the mistakes that I have made. The question would then need to be asked: Would I be truly me now if not for the mistakes, and the lessons I learned from those mistakes? I pray to you that I always remember that I am never going to be perfect; that I look for the lessons in my mistakes; and that I have compassion and forgiveness for those who make mistakes that harm others, including myself.

243 Attitude plays a big part in the success of a venture. And it is my attitude, either positive or negative, that will inform how I handle a problem that has shown up in my life. Yesterday, a very simple problem occurred as I was leaving the house. I became immediately irritated. I pray to you that, when I am feeling grumpy and am faced with a problem, I immediately acknowledge my grumpiness. If I am not able to focus on the source of my grump, then I should set it aside to attend to later. I also pray for a solution to the problem, that I might deal with it and get on with my day. It is without doubt that I am going to be facing problems every day, and often multiple times. It would be wise of me to adjust my attitude to deal with this reality.

244 Life is tough at times, and no matter who you are, you can never be permanently happy. It can be very hard to think about or respond to another person's pain when we ourselves are in pain. I pray to you that I am always aware that the person I am presently conversing with might not be at their best, because they are doing it tough; that no matter how hard life is at that moment, I always have compassion for others. For in helping another when they are down, I am helping myself.

245 There is nothing more galling, when my self-esteem is fragile, than when I come across someone who seems to think they are better than me. It is even more frustrating when I find that the reason is usually skin deep. I used to think in all honesty that, yes, there were people who were better than me—but then I realised that is just was not so. It was just that they were different! I pray to you that, if I come across someone to whom I feel I am superior, I smack myself to bring me to my senses. That I consider why I feel this way, and find a way to atone for the erroneous thought.

January

Volcano, Tanna Island, Vanuatu

246 Several years ago, someone asked me what my New Year's Resolution was. I said to them that I never made New Year's Resolutions because if, during the year, I worked on doing my best every day, then why was there a need? I pray to you that every day I will continue to look for ways to improve myself; to do things better; to look for ways to help the community; to learn more about myself, and to enjoy myself while I am doing it.

247 When I first took on this project, part of me felt that I might not be able to complete it. At that time, I didn't have a lot of belief in my creative ability. But as time passed and the prayers made it to the page, my Faith in my ability to complete this project began to strengthen. I pray to you with thanks, for I believe it was with your help that I was able to continue this undertaking. I also pray that I remember that you are always there to support me.

248 One of my greatest joys is discovering what is on the other side of the hill, or around the next bend. I love learning new things, not just about the land where I live, but about myself. Life does not have meaning without facing challenges. I pray to you that when life does challenge me, I have the courage to learn from it; that I don't walk away from the challenge because I fear the outcome; that I acknowledge that to know myself as fully as I am able, I have to challenge myself to stay on the path of self-discovery. You never know; there may be a gem hidden over the next hill.

249 There is nothing more exhilarating than the first rains that break a drought, or the first rays of sunshine after a flood. As with anything, too much of the one thing can become destructive. Not only does the earth need balance, but so do we. I pray to you that in all things, I look for a balance in my life. I know that I have an addictive personality, so I pray for that balance. I also pray that, as a society, we don't take or hoard more than we need and that all commodities are shared equally.

250 It is not until I have lost, or nearly lost something, that I truly realise how precious it is to me and my life. In many instances, I cannot stop the loss from happening but, in some, I do have a choice and will fight to keep it. I pray to you that I will always understand what is precious to me; and that I will work to keep it in my life. I also pray that I am respectful and supportive of worthy societal values.

251 We have all heard the saying: *'It ain't over until the fat lady sings.'* So how did this saying make it to Mother Mary's Uncommon Prayers? I don't know, except that it has been on my mind for the past twenty four hours. My understanding of this saying is that it comes out of the sporting arena, and means to concentrate until the last moment because, if your attention wavers, you could lose the activity that you are participating in. Whatever its meaning, it would to be one of the strangest sayings going around. Once again, I have no idea where this prayer is going. So today I will pray for all of the cuddly ladies out there (including myself), whether they can sing or not; that people look past their size and see the person underneath—a person with feelings, a unique individual with a beauty that goes more than skin deep.

252 Acceptance of my physical reality can at times be somewhat difficult, especially when I look out the window to see birds flying past, chirping their joy to the world. It may not look it, but they too have worries, just like us. I pray to you that when I am feeling unable to walk, I look at the times when I could and thank the Lord that I have the memory of that experience. I also pray for those who have never had the capability of even putting their foot to the ground. We all have our own crosses to bear and, as such, I should never presume the quality of another person's journey.

253 We can all make a difference to our world. We do not have to be a leader or a celebrity; it's just attitude. I pray to you that we all come to realise that we can make changes, and that it can start with just a small first step. I also pray that we have faith in our own ability to make that difference. I challenge myself that when I see a need, I be responsible and take action.

254 When I was growing up, I found it really hard to be my own person. The adults in my life wanted me to walk paths of their choosing. Whilst it was difficult for me to be respectful as a teenager, I found a way to follow my own unique path. I pray to you that I will always support others in their life paths; that I give advice when asked for it, but not direction, and that I listen to and am respectful of the paths that all choose. I have learned that following a path that someone else sets for you is a sure-fire way to find yourself travelling in the wrong direction—a direction that can leave you frustrated and unhappy.

255 There is great joy and often awe in watching a seed that we have sown grow into a strong sturdy plant, then bloom into a beautiful flower. It takes more than just one element for the plant to grow

to full bloom. The seed needs to be planted at the right time of the year; it also needs water, sun and the right kind of soil. For every single one of us, from plant to human and in between, we all need the right elements to bloom. I pray to you that we give each other the opportunity to achieve the potential that we have been born for; and that when we see a need in another, we stretch out our hand and offer that help.

256 Worrying about our future, no matter the issue, is something that most of us have difficulties with. It is also a waste of two of our precious resources—our energy and our time. Yes, our future may look bleak, but there is nothing we can do to change it except to prepare the best we can. I pray that I find ways to deal with my present worry; that I let go of the fear of my future; and that I work harder on living in my now. The challenge for us all is living for today and enjoying life, no matter the hardship.

257 One of the most important things for all of us to realise, in today's consumer driven society, is that the most precious thing in life costs more than money can buy, and is something that can never be possessed. Friendship is that priceless gift, and what it costs me is my time, energy and honesty to keep it healthy and joyous. It is worth it because, without it, I lose meaning and beauty in my life. I pray to you that I do not take any of my friendships for granted; that I take the time to nurture and care for them; and that I always treat them with the respect that they deserve. For it is through my friends that I learn about life, its meaning and who I am. And it is in friendship that I find the joy in living.

258 We all have likes and dislikes. For example, my brother loves baked cheesecake. If someone was to offer me cheesecake, I would only accept it if the dish it was on was gold-plated, and I could then keep the dish. One thing that bemuses, me about the like or dislike of anything, is how it can be so difficult to believe that someone can dislike something that we love so much. It can be a puzzling experience, to the point that, over the years, people will present the same things to us, thinking that we might change our minds. In some things, maybe; in cheesecake, never! I pray to you that, no matter how serious a like or dislike, we value each other's opinions; that we just don't push it; and that we accept that when it comes to preference, there is no right or wrong. We all just happen to be different … cheesecake and all!

259 I believe that one of the paths to enlightenment is in knowing that money will not gain me anything personally precious, including happiness. For me to attempt to use money in this way is missing the point of a meaningful life. I pray to you that you will help me to remember that to gain anything of value in my life, I will need to continue to be willing to work at it with my own hands. I also need to look at what is most precious to me in my life, and be willing to share it or give it away, so that I can bring true meaning to my journey through life.

260 For me, memories are the stories of my younger days; they show me the path of my past as I walked towards my future. These stories show me what was important, not just to me but to each of us in what we remember. Yesterday, I had a great experience with some family members. We went on a memory drive, to a place the family had not been to for some time. It was with joy and some sadness that we shared what we remembered. Some memories were as clear as a bell; some things I remembered not at all, as we reminisced on when we last walked this land as children, through all the changes in life through to today. I pray to you that I continue to remember that memories are a precious part of all of our histories; that we use them as a teaching tool to help remind us of the paths of past mistakes; and that we all take time to dip into the joy of our past—not because we want to get away from our present, but so we can reflect upon the work that it took to get us to where we are today.

261 With my busy lifestyle, I am often re-taught the lesson that the simple pleasures in life are often the best. This past weekend I was reminded, twice, of this humble truth. A Sunday drive … how often have we complained of those slow Sunday drivers? Well, I rediscovered how wise they can be in slowing down and enjoying the beauty surrounding them. I pray to you that I remind myself to slow down every day, not just on Sundays; and that I not only take time to enjoy life, but that I also share my enjoyment of life with others by inviting them to join me.

262 Today is a day that should bring us together as a nation. And yet it continues to deeply divide us. We all live in the shadows of our nation's history, a history that belongs to our ancestors but is now the responsibility of us all. I feel a deep compassion for our ancestors and the wrong that has been committed. I stand today, a daughter of this land, as I stand in unity with the First Peoples of our nation and of all nations. I pray to you that each and every one of us take the time to acknowledge and accept— not just the history of Aboriginal Australia, but of all Australians. Whatever our past, we are now one nation together. I also pray that we respect the path and pain of that history, and that instead of focusing on our past we turn and face our future together, so that we can find a path that addresses the needs of all of us.

263 Just because I cannot see an answer, it does not mean there isn't one. My life is not about giving up and letting life take its course, without me saying: *'Hey! Not gonna happen without a fight!'* I might not have an answer today, but I am gonna continue looking for ways that get the job done. I pray to you that, when I do find life hard and cannot seem to find a way through, I look outside the box to places that I have never tried looking before. The most important thing for me is actually not that I find the answer, but that I believe in myself; that I can find the right path even if it is not the answer that I thought that I was looking for.

264 From our very first dreams as children, we have pushed ourselves to be better. Whether our dreams be within the humanities, arts, science or other fields, each and every one of us has sought to step beyond our original programming. I pray to you that we all take the opportunity to reach out and dream dreams for the betterment of ourselves and humanity; and that as we follow our own creative paths, we find ways to help others follow theirs.

265 'They' say that patience is a virtue. Sadly, it is a virtue with which I struggle more often than I would like. There have been times when I stomp my feet so much, I worry about the strength of my boots. One of the lessons that I have had to relearn is that enlightenment is rarely instantaneous. I pray to you that when I am seen stomping my feet, people think that I am learning a new line-dance move; that I walk away from my frustration and just work on achieving zero expectations. I then need to take some time looking at the reality of what I was hoping to achieve. Sometimes I have to accept the fact that yes, it is possible, but it is gonna take more work that I thought. Am I ready for that? If not, expect more stomping in my future!

266 Have you ever found yourself completing the end of someone's sentence or story, before the other person has finished speaking? You then found yourself not listening, because you had made an assumption as to what the story was about? Regrettably, I have made this mistake way too often. I have found it to be a sure-fire way to cause confusion and sometimes hurt. I pray to you that you help me see the truth in every word and activity; to listen to the end and not to make assumptions.

267 Who in the whole world can we rely on to tell us the truth about ourselves? Well, I turn to my friends. During the years, we have shared many experiences together, and still to this day discover new things about each other. I pray to you that I never take my friends for granted; that I listen to them when they tell me a truth about myself, even if it is unpalatable; that I treat my friends like the precious gift that they are; and that no matter how long I may know someone, I will never presume to think that I know everything about them. I am learning new things about myself all the time, so obviously I am learning new things about them also.

268 How far will I go to defend the rights of someone to make their own decisions? It is a hard question, especially if the choice may harm the person making the decision. I pray to you that when I am faced with someone who is in this situation, I respect and support their right to make that choice.

269 I recently wrote: *'Premeditated wrong, to me, is a loss of personal enlightenment and is not healthy for the soul.'* I am talking about lying. We all have been known to lie. It is an uncomfortable issue to discuss but, according to science, it is impossible for a person not to lie. I personally don't think all lying is wrong; I love to embellish stories with my humour. But I am talking about lies that make us all uncomfortable; lies that in our hearts we know are wrong. I pray to you that I always challenge the honesty of what I say; that when I speak to others you give me the strength and courage to speak my truth; that I not harm others with false words. That I look for other ways, if I feel I need to lie to protect myself, or get a perceived need met.

270 Most of us are born into the love of family, and throughout our journey of life we sometimes find and are given other types of love. For some, it may be difficult accepting the joyous gift of love because we all know that, with the beginning of love, there is also an ending. I pray that when love crosses my path, I do not let the fear of loss lead me to reject it; that with courage, I open my arms, for it is in loving another that I will find the path to self-knowledge and love of self.

271 Procrastination is a skill that I have honed to a fine art over the years. If I do not want to do something, I have been known to invent 100 creative reasons why it cannot be done. I pray to you that, when I am faced with something that needs to be done, I just do it without making excuses; that if I honestly have problems, I ask for help; and if something needs to be done and I find myself out of my league, I swallow my pride and hand the project to another.

272 One of the realities that most fascinates me in this world is the uniqueness of each individual—not just our personalities, but also the paths that we walk professionally, creatively and how we spend our free time. The most important thing for me is that I am not only uniquely me, but that I continue to work on being the best me that I can. I pray to you for help in overcoming my fears, when facing challenges in my life; that I use these challenges to know myself better; and that I don't focus on just me; that I take the time to help others discover their own uniqueness.

273 No family is perfect, including my own. We all have problems that we have to deal with as we grow and live life. And although my family is not perfect, it is they that have given me the springboard into life. It is family who have helped support me as I have stepped out on my own and taken my first individual steps. I pray to you for all of those who do not have this kind of support, that they find others who can help them with this kind of care; I also pray for all parents, that they find it within themselves to help their children in their journey through life.

274 There are times when I wish to pray and there is silence in my mind. Meaningful prayers do not need words. I do not have to be eloquent. Prayer from the soul is what it is all about for me. I pray to you that if my words do not come, I have faith that you will hear the need within me; and that my heart speaks my thanks, whatever the outcome.

275 One of the most difficult things for me to do is sit in silence with myself. Why? Because I might hear a truth about myself that I do not wish to face. It doesn't matter how good I believe myself to be, I know that there are characteristics I am not comfortable with. There are things about myself I may not like, but this should not stop me from knowing myself fully. I pray to you for the strength to face that within myself that I do not like; to acknowledge it, and to work on being the best person that I can.

February

Out my back door

276 Today's prayer is one of thanksgiving. So, I pray to you giving thanks for my life and all that I have experienced and achieved; for my wonderful family, even though there are times we fight like cats and dogs; for the people in my life, even the ones I find difficult to like—they have helped me learn to be more respectful. I thank you for the beautiful planet that I live on— for helping me to see that I need to live a more sustainable life. I especially thank you for helping me deal with my mistakes— they have helped make me who I am today. Finally, thank you for the journey. It has not been easy but I am so grateful that I have been given the opportunity to live life.

277 The reality of life is that we are all going to experience loss. As we journey through life we begin to encounter grief, as we begin to lose the older members of our family and community, and more so as we get older ourselves. Some of us leave life much earlier, because of accidents and illness. Some live a life that is a real struggle. I pray to you that I accept my path in life, no matter how hard it may be; that I walk beside and help those who are doing it tough; and that I leave bitterness behind me. It is not an emotion worthy of any of us.

278 One of the difficult things, for me, is to forgive someone who has harmed me. When I feel this way, I look at the times I have hurt others, and think of the strength they have shown in forgiving the wrong that I have done them. I pray to you that I always find within me the ability to acknowledge and accept that I have and do hurt others, and that in those cases I need to seek forgiveness. And if I have harmed myself, I should find a way to right that wrong. It is often harder to forgive oneself than it is to forgive others, but we all need to remind ourselves that each of us are just as worthy of forgiveness.

279 Someone once asked me: 'How long does a prayer have to be, to be a prayer?' My answer was that a prayer became a prayer with your intention to pray. I pray to you that I remember that it is not the words that are important in prayer, it is the purpose behind them; to remind myself that prayer is not just words learnt by rote, nor a request to get my needs met but a conversation with the Divine; a place where I can speak my truth, and learn more about my Faith and who I am.

280 There are many irritants in life that cause me frustration. The challenge for me is in how to deal with them. Even though it can be satisfying smashing the kitchen plates, there is nothing more irritating then losing my cool over something that can usually be easily dealt with. I pray to you (for the sake of the kitchen plates) that I learn to deal with my frustration in a calmer way; that when I know that I am irritated, I learn to stop and step back; that instead of reacting in a way that is going to add more frustration, I learn how to deal with my annoyance in a more balanced way.

281 Jealousy is not a virtue that I strive for but I've been known to feel it at times. It is an ugly emotion, and one that says a lot more about me than the person I am jealous of. I pray to you that I am able to acknowledge that others are more gifted than I am in certain areas, and that they are deserving of their life path. This does not mean that they are any better. They are just walking that different path. And it is not my place to judge their path.

282 One of the most important gifts that I have been given is my life. My life matters to me and I must treat it with respect. I know that there are times when I stretch out my hand to those in need. Do I ever think of doing the same for myself? I pray to you that I take the time to look after me when I am in need; that I should politely walk away from those who try and deny me respect; and that I take to time to enjoy my own company. For it is in this time with me that I will get to know myself better.

283 One of my goals in life is to be the best person that I can. I know that this will not make me perfect, even though I will strive for it. I pray to you that all through my life, I continue to challenge myself; to question the actions that I take before they become blunders. That if I lose the plot and do wrong, I reflect on my activities, acknowledge my mistakes and seek forgiveness. Just because I am never going to be perfect is not a reason to give up. I need to acknowledge and accept that. I am human. I make mistakes. Deal with it!

284 There are a lot of pithy little sayings out there. While many of them have a kernel of truth, that truth can often be frustrating. For example, 'practice makes perfect.' We all have differing levels of skill, and no matter how much I practice at certain things, I know that I am going to continue to be just adequate. I pray to you that I acknowledge my limitations, and that my limitations should not be an excuse to not work at improving when I can. I may never be a world champion, but I know that I will be proud of myself if I have worked as hard as I can to be the best that I can be.

285 Yesterday, I was given the opportunity to re-learn the lesson that you cannot judge a person by their looks. I have to admit, to my chagrin, that I have had to re-learn this lesson way too often. I pray to you that, when I come across another person and begin to judge them, I stop and think about why I find the need to do this, and reflect on what it might say about me. And maybe, just maybe, if I meet this person in the future, I will discover what a gem this person is. *'I know not your path. How can I judge your footsteps?* (Jennifer Clarke, 2019)

286 There is this one line in a country song that I always related to, about being the biggest disappointment in the family. It wasn't until I reached adulthood that I began to understand that I was my own worst enemy. I would always be putting myself down, and was not successful because I never felt that I was good enough. I pray to you that I will in the future pay attention to other country songs about kindness and take it to heart—and that kindness is to me. I know I'm going to sound like a cracked record, but I need to remind myself that I am not perfect and am going to make mistakes; so, hey give myself a break and take some time to acknowledge all of the good things that I've done in life. And guess what? That is gonna take a while!

287 When I was young, I would look at an older person and think that they were from another species, as I did not think that we had a lot in common. I was respectful but, sadly, I did not work at getting to know them better. If only I knew then what I know now! The grace with which many of these people aged and the wisdom that they held would have been inspirational. I pray to you that I am as accepting of my path as I move into the twilight of my life; that I also accept I will not have the energy levels to participate in the activities I did when I was younger; and that I am, ironically, understanding of those young ones who look at me as if I am from another planet.

288 I had an experience yesterday that got me to thinking. I went to visit an older couple that I have known for some time. She looked unwell. I sat and talked to her and her husband for a few hours. At the end of my visit, she looked so much better. I pray to you, with thanks, for once again showing me that a simple act of kindness can be so powerful. Sometimes we don't even know that we have made a difference in someone's life. I also pray that when someone does make a difference to me, I tell them so and I thank them.

289 I recently heard someone say that suffering does not discriminate. Yes, I agree that it doesn't matter if you are rich and powerful, you can get a severe and even a terminal illness. But I also know that many such people will get better treatment than a poor person suffering the same illness. I pray to you that we all use whatever power that we have to help all of our sisters and brothers, whoever they may be, by fighting for equality in treatment. I also pray that it is not just health equality that we all fight for, but equality in all types of suffering. We all need to open our eyes to see that the suffering of one harms us all!

290 Yesterday I saw a most amazing sunset. A storm occurred about five minutes before the sun set. The sun appeared to become a red hole in the sky and then there was lightening. Wow! I grabbed my camera and prepared to try and capture this unique sight. It was not to be. While just a tad sad, I was not too disappointed, as it was one of the few images that would stay in my mind forever. I pray to you, with thanks, for the opportunity to see such beauty, and also for the opportunity to try and capture the image. While I did not capture the image, I was excited at the chance to try. So again, thank you.

291 How many times have any of us said 'yes' when we really wanted to say 'no?' Sometimes the answer has to be 'no,' but first I have to have the courage to stand up for myself. What damage have I caused when I did say yes? I pray to you that I continue to learn that my needs are just as important as another's; that I find the balance to care for myself, even while caring for others. And when I do say 'yes,' I make sure that I am doing it for reasons that speak to me, and not because I feel forced.

292 The level of a person's suffering is an individual experience, and we all suffer in different ways. Just because another's suffering appears to be so much worse than mine, it cannot be compared as neither person can live the other's suffering. I pray to you for the strength to cope with the suffering that I experience; that I do not invalidate my own because of another's path; and that I have compassion for all who suffer, including me.

293 I see my most important path in life as finding my own personal truth, while in balance with my Faith path. Both the truth of who I am, together with my Faith, is as individual as my personality. I pray to you that I understand that my truth and Faith is about me and for me, not another person; and the only wrong in all of these individual paths is if we lack respect for others.

294 It is true that our life can be hard and, yes, there are times when things can go drastically wrong. And yes, there will be suffering and grief, and it is without a doubt going to hurt. I pray to you that during these times, I acknowledge my loss and take time to explore this experience; that if I find myself not moving on, that I am indulging in that misery, then I investigate why I am finding it so difficult. It is true that loss and suffering will never leave me, but understanding and accepting this reality will help me find the motivation to walk more confidently into my future.

295 The older I get the more precious my time becomes. For me, without wanting to sound pretentious, sharing my time with others is also a precious gift. I pray to you that, while I acknowledge my time is important to me, I understand that I cannot hoard it. I also pray that I find ways of balancing the use of my time. So, while it is good to share and good to use for creative pursuits, it is also good to restore myself by seemingly wasteful activities.

296 From birth, we begin life being cared for, and then later in life we might be caring for others. It is not about controlling another's life; it is about being there for someone when they are in need. For those who do become long term carers, it takes a generosity of spirit and a great personal commitment to do so. We all need to care for each other in various ways, so I pray to you, with thanks, to all those long-term carers out there, and particularly for those who are finding it difficult at this moment. I also pray that they get their own needs met, while on this path.

297 We all have to make choices in our lives. At times, we don't have all the information we need, so the choice we make may not be right for that time. Then there are the decisions we make where we firmly believe that we are making the right choice. I pray to you for guidance in the future, that I have all of the information I need to make the choice that is right for me. I also pray that if there is another choice to be made, you please show me and I am open to it.

298 I have always found it difficult to forgive another when they have hurt me. And if they know that they have done wrong and won't apologise, then all bets are off. But I have to realise that forgiveness is not about the other person, it is about me letting go of the resentment and pain. The wrong that has been done is their responsibility, not mine. I pray to you that I learn that forgiving someone for harming me is not about letting them walk all over me. It is about letting go of my own angst. I also pray that those who have harmed another, including myself, find the strength to seek forgiveness from the person that we have harmed.

299 If I have difficulty in seeing the good in someone, how can I communicate positively with them? Yesterday, instead of contemplating what someone said to me, I got angry. I immediately dismissed the truth of their statement. I only heard the negative. I pray to you that, however I feel about a person, I show them the respect of hearing what they have to say; that I remember that we all have feelings and that we all have wisdom to share. It would be pretty stupid of me to ignore another's wisdom because I am uncomfortable with the source.

300 One of the greatest comforts in my life is knowing that I have a place that I call home: a place of warmth and safety; a place where I can let my hair down and be me. It is a gift that is precious, and one that I often take for granted—but that is also a gift, not having to worry about where I am going to sleep tonight. I pray to you, with gratitude, for the comfort of my home. I pray for those who do not have that luxury. I pray that we all, our society and our governments will find a way to solve this problem. This dilemma belongs to us all, and I give thanks to those who are already reaching out to folks in need.

301 I always thought that as I got older I would not have as much to learn. I now believe in that adage that: *'The more you know, the more you don't know.'* (Aristotle). I also believe that if you've stopped learning, then you've stopped living. So, I pray to you that I will always remain inquisitive; that I never lose the joy of discovering new things for myself; and that I will always want to journey to see what is on the other side of the hill. It does not matter if someone else has been there first, seen it first, learnt it first. To me, it is important that I learn through my own experiences.

302 One of the definitions of fear for me is anticipation of something that may or may not happen, whether in the present or in the future. And as I get older, often that fear is about my health. I pray to you that if I am truly afraid for my health, then I work on it in the present. And yes, there are times when my path is going to be rough. I pray for the strength and the courage to accept my present and future path.

303 The following simple prayer came quickly last evening, after having lived through a tremendously stressful day. I pray to you—help me to get out what needs to come out. Help me to learn what needs to be learnt. Help me to accept what is the truth, even if it is a tough truth.

March

Two leaves together

304 Have you ever thought about the people you talked to, on any given day, and wondered if you made a difference in their life? It could have been as simple as seeing someone on the other side of the road and crossing to say g'day. We never know the influence we have on someone's life, just by a simple act of kindness. I pray to you that I make it an aim in my life to consciously go out of my way to be kind and attentive to all those I come in contact with.

305 One of the most frustrating things in life is when I have organised my timetable and someone I was relying on pulls out, because of their own agenda. There is absolutely no point in becoming irritated at a situation that cannot be changed. That is a waste of time and energy. I pray to you that during these times of frustration, I learn to go with the flow; to relax and to look outside the box to find other ways to achieve what I set out to do.

306 One only has to look at the diversity of the animal kingdom to realise the amazing uniqueness of each individual that walks this planet. How we become those unique personalities can be explained not just by genetics but our culture, environment, experiences and how we were raised. And even then, siblings who walked very similar paths to adulthood can have completely different personalities, and often different beliefs from each other. I pray to you that we all find joy and acceptance in our own uniqueness; that as we walk the path of life, we study our differences, and don't just accept that we are a finished product that never changes; that we acknowledge and encourage the changes within ourselves as we mature and experience life.

307 For me, memories are not there to re-live as something I have lost. I see my memories as a celebration of my path in life, and those who walked beside on the journey. I pray to you for your assistance in helping me comprehend the things that I have missed in my past; that my memories continue to enlighten me about my life journey; and that I continue to realise that I do not have memories just to re-live the pain of loss, but the joy I have had in living life and the people that helped to form my life.

308 We all suffer from tragedies in our lives which change us to varying degrees. As we know, tragedy is a part of our journey of life. I pray to you that when facing my own personal tragedies, I realise I do not have to face it alone; and that I don't compound the tragedy by remaining knocked over by it, but find a way to get back on my feet and continue the journey.

309 I sit here bereft of creative thoughts, disappointed in my inability to put words together. I pray to you, within this silence, to acknowledge I need no words to communicate my thoughts, needs or thanks; and to also recognise that my presence is often more important than words. At times, it is in the silence when we can best hear what is in our hearts.

310 No matter our experiences in life, we all have a story to tell and wisdom to pass on. For with every experience, we learn something new about life. I pray to you we all come to realise that, no matter who we are or where we come from, each and every one of us has a unique story to tell. What would be sad would be if we felt that it was not worth sharing.

311 There is a crossroads about one kilometre, as the crow flies, from the river where I used to swim as a child. If I was to take any one of the four directions at the crossroads, they will eventually get me home. Two directions are pretty easy roads with few potholes. The other two eventually become dirt, and are pretty rough going in places. For me these crossroads and where they take me are symbolic of my journey through life. So, I pray to you that I will always see the value in taking all four routes, even the toughest one home; that I will investigate other roads that also might lead me home; and I will always be on the lookout for things I've never seen before. I also pray that I am open to surprises, because sometimes where I have been aiming for is not where I've ended up.

312 How many excuses have I made in the past that I've lived to regret? We all make excuse to get out of activities we don't want to do … I'm too tired; it's too wet; too hot; too dry; feeling sick. Whatever excuse I give, I need to remember that I will never be given the opportunity to experience this moment in time again. I pray to you that, before I walk away from an opportunity, I ask for clarity; to study it and ask myself how important would it be for me to experience this moment. And even though the excuse may be valid, that I also ask myself: 'If it is right for now, then shouldn't I pray for the motivation to do it?'

313 Sometimes I feel as if all I do is trudge up hills in bad light, with the wind blowing in my face and the rain thumping on my head.

There are times in life when all I want to do is just sit down and give up. What do I think is gonna happen then? Well, I reckon one of two things—I'm gonna have to start all over again, or I am going to miss out on something that was truly worth the suffering of climbing that hill. I pray to you for the strength to carry on when times are tough; and if I am not able to continue, then the acceptance that living this present experience was not meant to be at this time.

314 There is no right or wrong place to pray … although I would strongly recommend not dropping to your knees in the middle of the Harbour Bridge during peak hour. There is no right or wrong way to pray. And you don't have to be in a certain mood. Sometimes I pray and the noise in my head is so distracting, it feels like I'm at a T20 cricket match. None of this matters. The only thing that matters is my intent. So, I pray to you in thanks, with joy in my heart for your presence in my life; for your understanding that my prayers will never be perfect. I also request a little help in achieving stillness and silence when I need that in my prayer.

315 If I don't believe in myself, who is gonna believe in me? How am I going to get anything done; how am I gonna set goals, get a job, learn new skills or be the person that I have always dreamed of becoming? I pray to you for clarity, to see the strength I have within myself, to be able to achieve the goals that I have always dreamed of accomplishing. I do have that strength, and it starts with one small step; and that is self-belief.

316 Preventing myself from being injured or hurt is important for my own wellbeing. There are some things I would not do because I know they are too dangerous. And yet, there are some adrenalin junkies out there that live on the edge. What is important, though, for all of us, is that by trying to stay safe, we don't cease living. I pray to you for the strength and self-awareness to acknowledge my limitations; to realise that I do not have to climb mountains, drive fast cars or jump out of planes to find the fun in life. What is important to me is finding what brings me joy, not trying to outdo someone else!

317 There are times in my life that I do not feel you within it. This is usually when I am doing it tough and I do not believe in myself. I am poorer for this and, at these times, I lack light for my path. I pray to you when I need you most in my life, that I find the strength to open my spirit to your healing presence. For without you, I am less and cannot be fully me.

318 Everyone's character is challenged in the face of grief, disaster and struggle. We are all tested to find the power within ourselves, to seek an answer and find a way to cope with what we are facing. I pray to you that as I face these trials, I see them as a way to learn about myself; a crossroads, if you will, where I have to face the decision of where my journey will take me next.

319 One of the things that I have noticed while travelling through life is that many people appear stronger, happier and more balanced when they have a loved one beside them. I have also discovered that when you have a friend alongside you who believes in you, you are more likely to succeed. I pray to you with thanks, for all the people in my life that I know care for me and love me. I also pray with thanks that I can be that for others. I have also found in my journey through life that while I cannot possess another, their friendship and care is more precious than anything that I could ever own.

320 I have found over the years that patience and I don't often go together, but can lead to frustration. To judge how unbalanced I am, on any given day, the best exercise is to ring a government department seeking assistance. I pray to you with thanks, for helping me see the humour in the situation; for learning that preparation is a good calming tool … For me, this means having something else to do while I am waiting; and if preparation does not work, don't take out my frustration on the other person. I have no idea the pressures that they are under. Be my best self and treat them politely and with kindness.

321 We often hear people say after they saved someone: 'I'm not a hero. I just did what had to be done.' When faced with a situation where a person puts their own life in danger to rescue another, we are truly seeing the best in this person. I pray to you with thanks, for all the humble and giving people who have put themselves in danger for others. Only a few of us have been given the opportunity to show our best in this way, but it is my belief that we all have the hero/ine within us.

322 Sadly, I have learnt through experience that one of the greatest mistakes in communicating positively with another is to make an assumption about that person. How can I see the truth? I pray to you that before I talk with anyone, even if I think I know them, I do so with a clean slate and leave my assumptions at the door.

323 One of the greatest joys in the world is to watch children play. The greatest responsibility of every conscious being on the planet is to help children grow into their potential, with the least amount of scarring. We all have that responsibility, whether we are a parent or not. I pray to you that we all realise the damage we can cause an impressionable mind with just a few wrong words. Help me to live by the following motto: *'Spoil children not with material gifts, but with the knowledge that they are loved.'* (Jennifer Clarke *Thru My Eyes & My Words Too* 2018)

324 What is more important: making your mark in life, or helping others on their journey? My greatest goal is to know myself as fully as I am able. This is the mark I wish to make in life and to do this, I have to interact with others. I pray to you that I will always see that in helping others, wisdom will be gained; that in helping others, I will become stronger and more self-aware; and that in helping others, I will be able to achieve more of my potential. For in showing a generosity of spirit and reaching out my hand, I am living my best self.

325 When I was younger, I used to believe that no one would like me if I did not do things for them or give them gifts. I no longer believe that lie. One good thing to come out of it, though, was that it reinforced my generous nature. My generosity is one of the parts of my personality that I admire. I pray to you that, when we realise something we believe about ourselves is a lie, we reflect on it then let the lie go. We need to ask ourselves what good can be found in this lie? I pray that we can all see the good in who we are.

326 When you think of the term 'miracle,' many people think of a huge event like the parting of the Red Sea. My thoughts are not so grandiose. When I think of the impossible happening, no matter how small, then to me that is a miracle. I recently lost something that I thought I would never find again. I prayed for help and it was in my hand within a short period of time. That might not seem like a miracle to others, but it stopped me dead in my tracks and had me saying a prayer of thanks. I pray to you to help us see that we have miracles happening to us all the time, no matter how big or small. I know not the reason why there is so much pain and suffering in life, or why many of our prayers appear not to be answered. What I do know is that every single one of us walks the path of pain and suffering in some way. I pray that you also help me at these times, to have strength and belief and Faith; that you walk with me always and that you are at the foot of my own personal cross during my need.

327 I have begun to notice that when many people retire, they take up an activity that they never had time for previously. It is often in the creative arts and they can discover that they are very good at it. I wonder if they regret waiting so long to start using and refining this skill. Our lives are so short and regrets can leave bittersweet feelings and memories. I pray to you that when we are faced with an opportunity in our lives, you help us to find a way to grab it and make it happen. We need to remember that we may never pass this way again.

328 Today we honour the death of Christ on the cross. During this time of the Christian Calendar, I meditate on how this day and the journey of the cross applies to me in my Faith and personal life. I focus on it in two ways—Jesus' and Mother Mary's experiences. I see Jesus in agony, and admire his courage and grace in continuing to move forward on this path. And then there is his mother, witnessing the painful journey of her son. She does so with amazing dignity. I pray to you with thanks for all that you have done for humanity through the living of your life. I pray that when I am experiencing my own personal journey of the cross, even though I am in pain and possibly angry at life, that I feel you walking beside me, acknowledging me and witnessing my journey. I also pray that your presence gives me strength, to help me overcome my anger and accept my present path.

329 I am led to believe that there was a time in my life when as soon as I opened my eyes of a morning, I jumped out of bed with joy and energy, ready to start my day. Personally, I think that is a rumour, without any foundation in fact! Most of my adult life I have had to drag myself out of bed, and it would have been at least an hour before an intelligent thought passed through my brain. Have I mentioned that I really dislike morning people? Now if dragging myself out of bed is the only problem I have during the day, then I am a lucky person. Why? I have that warm bed to get out of. I pray to you with thanks for the joy of that bed. I pray for the motivation to see the positive in my life, every morning I wake. I also pray with thanks for what I have achieved in my life, and what I still have in front of me to achieve.

330 When I was a child, my mother told me that the sun danced on Easter morning because God was so excited that Jesus had risen from the dead. Then mum would pick each of us up so that we could have a better look. I never ever (well, until I got older) related the dancing of the sun to Mum's jiggling me while she held me. Many years later, this memory still brings a smile to my face. The love of a mother is an amazing and powerful force. I pray to you with deep thanks for the gift of my mother and all mothers, especially yourself; for the self-sacrifice of Jesus; and for the selfless sacrifice of all those who gave of themselves to help others in need.

331 When the finish line is in sight, a number of things could happen. You could sprint through with your hands raised in joyous victory. Or maybe you could stroll quietly through, with your head bowed in thanks. Or you could possibly stumble and never reach the finish. Maybe someone is on the same path as you and they slow to help you to your feet. I pray to you with thanks for witnessing my journey thus far; and to help me see that I do have the skills and strength to complete my journey. I thank you for your support.

332 Why do I continue to work towards a goal when I know that the chances are slim to none of achieving it? I reckon that there are two reasons—the journey, itself, and the belief in a possible miracle. I pray to you that, whatever goal I think may be impossible, I do not give up trying. The chance may be remote, but I reckon the journey will teach me more about myself and lead me on a path that I never thought of taking before.

333 We have all been given a certain amount of time to live on this earth. Much of that time is spent in the service of earning a living; in relationship with others; achieving personal goals; enjoying life. Time is a gift and a precious commodity. I often hear people (including myself) state 'what a waste of time!' As far as I am concerned, however we live time, it cannot be wasted. I pray to you that when it comes to my use of my time, I learn to accept my physical limitations; that I learn I am not a slave to time and that I take some of that time to relax and enjoy life.

April

Easter Cross, All Saints Catholic Church, Kempsey

334 Through the Immaculate Conception you gave birth to your son, and your Faith did not waiver. You watched him grow to manhood and shake the religious beliefs of the Middle East, and your Faith did not waiver. You watched as they condemned him to death then followed him as he carried his cross through Jerusalem, and yet your Faith did not waiver. You stood at the foot of the cross and watched, powerless and in agony, as your child died on that cross; and still your faith did not waiver. You were always a strong presence in the life of your son, Jesus. You trusted in his life path and because of that trust, your Faith did not waiver. I pray to you with gratitude, for your existence in the life and history of this planet. I pray with thanks for the strength of Faith you displayed, which has inspired so many. Thank you for that inspiration in my life and Faith, and in the life and Faith of so many.

335 I have never believed that the pain in my life is caused by my previous infractions. But I do believe that the cycle of life includes luck, and on this particular path I have lucked out. That does not mean that I have not been lucky on other paths. We are all going to suffer during our lives, some more than others. How we deal with it is part of our life journey. I pray to you for help, that all of us may open our eyes to the knowledge that part of our responsibility is to reach out our hand in kindness to those who are suffering; not because we are going to need help ourselves one day, but because we genuinely want to help that person to heal and to achieve.

336 If I do not honour the uniqueness of all, then I am not being true to my own personal journey. I pray to you that I treat all with respect, for in dishonouring another, I dishonour myself. I also pray that I am honest in all my deliberations with others. Also, please help me to remind myself that we all have the right to speak and be heard.

337 There are times when I think that my suffering is unique, and nobody could possibly understand the pain I am in. This is an arrogant thought and one I believe to be wrong. Nobody needs to have walked exactly the same path to understand another's life experience, their pain or their fear. I pray to you that when someone reaches out their hand in compassion, you gift me with the humility to accept it. The truth is that compassion offered does not need understanding. Compassion is the evidence of that person's path.

338 I sit here on a beautiful autumn day and wonder how I made it this far. I survived an uncountable number of accidents, which culminated in stitches, burns, contusions, concussions and broken bones. My mother swore that all of her grey hair came from me. I sit here today, uniquely me, because of my experiences and mistakes in those long ago years. But I am also me because of the indulgence of my family, as they mostly stood back and allowed me to walk my own path. I pray to you that when faced with encouraging the growth of another, I stand back and support them on the path of their choosing. I also pray for the wisdom to know when to provide guidance and when to keep my mouth shut.

339 I cannot say this enough—one of the greatest gifts we have been gifted with in this life is that of friendship. Last night, I got a text from a friend & cousin who told me that I was amazing and it was an honour to know me. I had been doing it tough for a little while and to get that message out of the blue … well, it was priceless. I pray to you with thanks for my friend, and for all my friends; and I pray that life is treating them kindly. I also pray that you help open my eyes to the possibility that all those around me have the potential to be a friend. But whatever they are to me in life, I need to remember to treat all equally and with kindness.

340 Many years ago, William Shakespeare coined the phrase: *'All the world is a stage.'* I would have to agree with him. We all wear masks; at times our faces belie what is really going on inside of us. Why is it that, at times, we cover up what we are truly feeling? I pray to you that when I am wearing a mask, you aid me in realising that I am doing so. I also pray for help in gaining insight as to why I feel that need. I acknowledge that none of us can stand alone, and that awareness might help me take off my mask and trust another.

341 One of the things that I really enjoy is watching someone use their skills to improve their life, and the lives of those around them. Whether at work, play or at home, we all have the need to put our stamp on our environment. I pray to you that we all have the opportunity to live our lives in the way that we wish; that we are able make our mark on our part of the world, and that in doing so, we do it respectfully.

342 On this cool beautiful autumn morning, I look into the hills of the Great Dividing Range, where I grew up, and the memories of my childhood come flooding back. One of those memories is of walking across the paddock and up to the road to catch the bus. We all had to carry our school shoes, because mum wanted them to last as long as possible. In summer this was not so difficult, but in winter it was rather chilly on the toes. Being a child who was rather creative in thinking outside of the box, I decided that the warm fresh cow pats dotted about the paddock would come in handy on those cool mornings. The only problem was how to clean my feet before I put my shoes and socks on! All bets were off with the shoes, though, if there was a thick frost. You see, the shoes were fantastic for skating across the ground. I wonder if that was where the term 'skating on thin ice' came from. As a kid, I was sure told that a lot! Anyway, I pray to you in thanks for the smile I wear this morning and for the great memories that I possess. I pray that all children, as they grow up, are able to gain wonderful memories that will bring them strength and joy as they grow older. It is my prayer that all children are afforded the opportunity to be children. No child should grow up too quickly.

343 If I see someone doing a job in a different way to what I would normally do, what is my first thought? I would like to think that I would take the time to investigate how they completed the task, to see if their way is better, but often my thought is that my way is the best way to do it. I pray to you requesting your assistance, to help me look humbly at myself and the way I live life, and accept that there is more than one way to accomplish a task. My way of dealing with something might be right for me, but it might not be right for another. I also pray that you help me to remain open to constructive encouragement.

344 One of the things I hate most in life is hurting someone. One of the most frustrating things in life is hurting someone through misunderstanding. In these circumstances, where I know that I have unintentionally harmed someone, I have found that reconciling is much more important than my possibly dented pride. Apologising about a perception can open the door to improving my relationship with that person. I pray to you for your help in accessing my humility, so that I am able to apologise when I am in the wrong; and the strength to reconcile a hurt that I have inadvertently caused.

345 When someone hurts me in what they say or do, do I presume that it was a misunderstanding? Or that they meant to do it? It is a hard one, and I hope that I would give them the benefit of the doubt. But there are times when it happens from the same person once too often. Sometimes another's life path will intersect with mine and leave misunderstanding and pain. I know not why they have come into my life, except to teach me something about myself. What lesson that person has to learn has nothing to do with me. It is not for me to figure out why they did what they did, but to understand why I reacted/responded the way I did. I pray to you that you help me gain awareness, so that I make no assumptions; to be respectful and not respond in kind. I also pray for the strength to walk away if I am being harmed. I am not required to turn the other cheek; I am obliged to look after myself as my life is my responsibility.

346 One of the greatest healing properties on the face of the planet is that of laughter. I find there is nothing more joyful than hearing the uplifting sound of someone having fun. When I laugh, it is a bit like washing myself of all my negative emotions. I know that I will not always be happy, and sometimes I feel that a smile is a million miles away. I pray to you that when I am feeling down, I ask for your help to access the happy within my soul; and that when I come across others who are sad, I find ways to touch them with the healing power of laughter.

347 One of the most breathtaking scenes on the whole of this planet can only ever be seen in full dark, and that is the night sky. While taking in the immensity of this view, I have no trouble believing in a Power greater than myself... the Power I call God. Nor do I have trouble believing in miracles. But one of the things that I feel the most while taking in this wondrous sight is that I feel comfortable and at home. I also feel humbled—not at how small I am, but at how little I really know. I pray to you that when I am feeling arrogant for whatever reason, you remind me of the night sky and how awe-inspired it is; that when my Faith is rocky, you motivate me to take a walk in the dark, to remind myself of my place in the miracle that is life.

348 For one reason or another, there is not one of us on the face of the planet who has not had to give up on a dream. Over the years, I have had to let go of more than one dream. From that very first loss of a dream, which I thought was a disaster, to now, where I have the awareness to understand that as I change, my dreams will have to change. I haven't stopped dreaming. I have just found more appropriate dreams. I can no longer dream of being a camp-drafter, but I can cheer my cousins on and take the occasional good photo. So, I pray to you that, whatever my path, you give me the courage to continue to dream and to achieve. My body may continue to challenge me, but my mind still fires the creative spirit within. To let go of my dreams is to give up on living. That I will never do! Following my path and using the example of Mother Mary, I will continue to dream.

349 I sit here today on a wildly different path than the one I thought I would be on when I was a kid. To my mind back then, there was no indication that I had the potential to be what I am today. Does this mean that I have to give thanks for the potholes and mistakes that I have experienced in my life? I think that it might. Come to think of it, I believe I need to reflect on the word 'mistake.' I don't think that it is the right word in anyone's vocabulary. Maybe I should call it slamming-the-brakes-on-and-taking-a-sharp-left. Shrug! If making a mistake is what helped get me where I am today, how can I call it a mistake? I pray to you first with thanks in helping me to gain my present path; and for bringing me to an awareness of my present potential. Please help me to choose wisely any future paths I need to take.

350 In my memory, I have never been called pretty or good-looking. Thinking this whimsical thought yesterday got me wondering how I felt about that. I was a little bemused… You know, I've never given it a second thought, or even a first, for that matter. It is not anything that I am really interested in. If someone said I was pretty, I'd be wondering what they are on about. I think it may be because I am more interested in what is going on inside myself and in others: our character; what makes us tick. Who we are is more important to me. I pray to you that I will always look beyond the cover of a person to their heart; that I help those I come into contact with to see that what is truly important about themselves is the beauty within. Yes, I understand that making yourself look attractive is important at times, but I would like to note that ugly has character too!

351 There are times when I have had to let dreams go because I knew that there was no way that I could achieve them. And then there were the ones that I let go too soon, because I didn't take the time to look at it from all angles, or even think of changing the parameters. As I get older, somewhat disabled and maybe a tad grumpier, I am going to have to think outside the box more often. I pray to you for the creative nous to look at ways of achieving the dreams that may seem impossible; that I don't throw them away because it just seems too hard. And I pray again … to swallow my pride and ask for help. It can be the difference between achieving the dream and gnashing my teeth.

352 No matter how often I meditate I don't think I will ever be truly skilled at it. I sit here as much in stillness as I can, aspiring to silence of the mind, then find myself thinking about a problem, reliving a memory or even daydreaming. One would think that after so many years of practice, I would have it down pat. And then I've discovered that if my mind won't close down it is usually for a reason. I have since learnt a few lessons when I have focused on the thoughts that stuck in my mind. I pray to you every day for the strength and motivation to sit in quiet contemplation of life and the Divine; and to work on achieving focus and openness. But I also need to remember that I don't have to be perfect in prayer to touch the Divine.

353 I ask myself today what in my life would cause me to abandon self-interest. I know that many incredibly brave people have answered this question with their lives. And many have done it without thought. Some have even forfeited their sanity. All have stood in front of danger and sacrificed their then present reality for the sake of another and/or a deep-seated principle. All of these people are worthy of the status of hero/ine. Today I pray to you with gratitude for all of those who have donned the slouch hat. May the echo of their self-sacrifice, generosity, Aussie spirit and service to their country be an example to all down the ages.

354 On Anzac Day, I reflected on our heroic slouch-hat warriors. Today I pray for those hero/ine's who walk among us every day, who dance with danger when they don their uniform. I thank you for all that you do and for being a living example of the strength of the human spirit. I pray for the safety of those who often work in danger; for those who have been injured in service to us all. I pray for healing of their mind, body and spirit. Truly these brave human beings are worthy of the greatest of respect, for placing their most precious gift, their lives, on the line for us.

355 Recently I was talking to someone I had not seen in a long time. After a while, she stated that: 'I had not changed a bit.' After many years of personal development and self-reflection, I did not know if I should have been frustrated or insulted. But then I realised that they were not really looking at me but at the package—the clown; the storyteller; the one seemingly always looking for fun. I also realised that meeting that person took me emotionally back to the time when I last saw her, and my personality seemed to devolve to that point in time. I pray to you for the strength to help me honour and respect my own personal journey, by being myself as I am today; that I also honour that person's journey and where they have come from. Change is sometimes not obvious but our learned wisdom is. I need to trust my path and believe in who I have become.

356 The death of a significant other in my life gives me the opportunity to meditate on the journeys that we took together. Their life, and what they taught me when our paths crossed, gives me the opportunity to reflect on how that person touched me, and to give thanks for their presence in my life. I pray to you with thanks for all of those who have crossed my path; who have made an impact in my life; and I give thanks for their life. I also give thanks for all of those that they have touched during their journey on this planet. I pray that their memories will help lighten their grief.

357 One of the greatest gifts that I have been given is the strength and love of family. Granted, there have been some great fights down through the years and yes, we are not perfect. But I do know that when I am doing it tough, I can turn to family for help. In our imperfection, I know that it is family that can hurt us the most. Through my path in life, I have realised that none of us have all the answers and that we all make mistakes, many of them made in innocence. I have learned again and again that we all try to do the best that we can. I pray to you with gratitude for the beautiful family that I have been gifted with; for those who do not have family, that they are gifted with many true friends; to remember that one of the best tools we have in healing misunderstanding is the simple apology. I also pray that when faced with a difficult reality, we all work on doing the best we can for each other, and for ourselves. This for me is what life is all about.

358 One of the lessons that I have been rather slow in learning during my lifetime is the lesson of the lost opportunity. Whether it is a visit to a relative or friend; a project; a particular photograph; or even a promise that I made that I never got around to. How many times have I told myself that I am going to come back and do it later? And then the situation changes and later never comes. I pray to you seeking forgiveness for any harm I may have caused, if I have let an opportunity go; for the motivation to attend to an opportunity as quickly as I can in my now and my future; and to reflect on what I've lost so that I can learn from that loss.

359 One of the hardest things to do in the world is to sit and watch a loved one suffer, knowing that you are powerless to do anything. This suffering can call into question our Faith, and raise many other questions. The main one being Why? Why has God let this happen? Why did God not save them? I do not know if anyone has ever satisfactorily answered any of these 'Why' questions. But I do believe that this is not God's question to answer. I know that these are questions that I do not have an answer for, nor will I ever in this lifetime. But strangely, these questions strengthen my Faith and help give my life meaning. I pray to you for all of us, as we all suffer on our life's journey. I pray that the strength of our Faith and those we love will bring us comfort during these times, that are sadly part of life. I also pray that I never give up on trying to bring enlightenment to these seemingly answerless questions; for one day I might be able to find a truth that I can understand.

360 Love is the most precious commodity on the face of the planet. Love can give us the strength to be a better human being; to travel paths we never thought were possible. The loss of love, through death, is a most painful experience. I pray to you that I find the courage to continue to love, and to be open to love, even when I know that I will lose that love in the future; that I acknowledge that I cannot achieve my full potential without the power of love in my life.

361 In my opinion, one of the most painful and incapacitating illnesses that humanity faces today is that of unstable mental health. I have found through living it that, in its most debilitating state, mental illness strips you of who you are and leaves you powerless and without strength to participate fully in life. While unwell I believed that I had nothing to offer family or community. I literally felt like I was at the Gates of Hell. My suffering mind perpetrated the lie that I was not good enough; that nothing I have done or am doing in my life was good enough and no matter what anyone else said I was definitely a failure. I didn't want to talk about how I felt because I knew that I was always going to be a failure and nothing and no words would change that. I also felt ashamed that I was such a failure. At that time, I lived my life on an island, isolating myself because I did not want my family and friends to see how big a failure and disappointment I was; I believed that others were judging me as not good enough.

My illness took away my ability to see the truth … that my mind was perpetrating a lie that made me feel like a useless human with nothing to offer. I truly believed this. Why is it that we can understand and accept the pain and disability of a broken leg and yet we cannot understand and accept the pain and disability when our mind is unwell and cannot think in a balanced way?

But the truth is that yes, I am/we are good enough and I/we will no longer allow that lie to control my/our life anymore.

I pray to you Mother Mary that the fog of these lies is removed from our mind and that we find the strength to face the truth that whoever we are or are becoming, and what we aim to achieve, we are good enough and will always be good enough. It is also important to remember that we all make mistakes. Let us find the wisdom in the learning and find the strength to continue to strip the lies from our life and to find the truth that the lies have been covering. If someone offers me a hand to help me walk away from my Gates of Hell I pray that I am smart enough to take it. I pray with all my heart that I don't continue to perpetrate lies that take away from my truth and happiness. And one thing for all of us to remember is that we have all walked a somewhat similar path at times during our lives. If there is a chance that our experiences may help smooth this painful path for another then yes we must hold out our hand. Let us help each other get to our feet and walk that healing path. For I will and now do believe that I was good enough yesterday; I am definitely good enough today; and will be into my future.

362 One of the things that means so much for me and that I pray a lot for is individual potential. It is my belief that all adult humans are responsible for the nurturing of human potential, not only their own but that of their children and the community. I pray to you that we all respect each other; give each other positive feedback; allow others to freely express themselves, and acknowledge the good that we all do. There is nothing more joyful than seeing the birth of someone's potential and knowing that you had even a small hand in it. It begs the question—what footprint will this person leave? Indeed, what footprint will any of us leave?

363 During the last several years, I have discovered that the possibility of losing an opportunity is a powerful motivator for me. I found that if I stopped doing something because it hurt, I was tired, or for whatever reason I might have thought up at the time, then I might never have the opportunity to do that activity again. I pray to you that, no matter how hard life can become, I will not stop doing what I enjoy doing, or what needs to be done. I also pray that everyone is able to find their own motivational tool, to help them achieve positive outcomes in their lives.

364 There are times when I am so tired that I cannot think straight. At these times, I have found that no matter the provocation, it is wise to keep my mouth firmly closed, as I may say something that I will regret. The tiredness may also have me making assumptions, which end up being just that. I pray to you that during these times, if I am in this situation, you help me to keep my mouth closed, no matter what the irritation; and that if I do open my mouth, I have the grace to apologise for any unwise words I might have said.

365 It is very hard at times to believe in my writing ability, when the page is clean and my mind is empty. I need to say, though, that there have been very few times when I have needed to pray for help during this past year. So, simply I pray with gratitude to Mother Mary for the inspiration to write the prayers for this Project. It is my belief that, without your help, the Project would not have been completed. I also thank those who supported me during the past year, especially those who told me that this Project was worthy.

The last words written on the final page of a book are usually:

'The End'

But for this project, it is not the end. It is just a completed part of the journey, and the beginning of a change in direction…

Index

A

Acceptance – 19, 99, 149
Achievement – 237
Acknowledging my faith – 116
Addiction – 7
Advice – 176
Aging – 215, 287
Ancestors – 57
Answers – 263
Anticipation – 131
Anzacs – 353
Apology – 39, 344
Approaching death – 229
Arrogance – 87, 180
Assumptions – 159, 266, 322, 364
Attitude – 56, 155, 179, 243
Australia Day – 262

B

Bad mood – 83
Balance – 249
Beauty – 4
Beauty within – 350
Belief in self – 62, 75, 247
Belief – 33
Behaviour – 184
Being my best – 283
Being prepared – 190
Be myself – 86
Best way – 343
Birthday – 28, 141
Bizarre activity – 196
Brokenness – 134

C

Caring – 296, 335
Celebration – 228
Challenges – 225
Change – 103, 122, 183, 208, 216
Children – 2, 51, 192, 323
Choices – 103, 210, 297
Christmas – 218, 239
Coincidence – 31
Communicating – 299
Comparison – 187, 202
Compliments – 13
Concentration – 8
Confusion – 105
Contrasts – 101
Control – 50
Cranky – 191
Creative – 47
Crosses to bear – 192, 252
Crossroads – 311
Culture & Belief – 235

D

Death – 9, 88, 356
Decisions – 268
Depression – 10, 26
Difference – 126, 173
Different – 81
Disappointment – 5, 128
Discomfort – 207
Disliking others – 170
Disrespect – 206
Down times – 199
Dreams – 110, 264, 351

E

Earth – 200, 221
Emotions – 65
Environment – 55, 64, 152
Equality – 289
Excuses – 195, 226, 312
Exhaustion – 94

F

Faith – 85, 153, 172, 240
Failure – 18, 74, 140, 209
Falling star – 14
Family – 15, 78, 231, 273, 357
Fat Lady – 251
Fear – 16, 158, 302
Finding meaning – 49
Finish line – 331
Fires – 17
Flexible plans – 90
Focus – 23, 44, 175
Forgetfulness – 113
Forgiveness – 278, 298
Friendship – 71, 197, 257, 267, 319, 339
Frustration – 120, 280
Fun – 32

G

Generosity – 107
Giving – 66
Giving my life meaning – 234
Goals – 127, 332
Good fortune – 63, 97
Good sense – 142
Go with the flow – 305
Grief – 96

H

Healing – 151
Help – 143, 167
Helping others – 233, 324
Hero/ine – 98, 321, 354
History, accepting – 193
Home – 132, 300
Homeless – 36
Honour – 336
Humour – 198, 213
Hurting others – 163

I

'If only' moments – 191
Imagination – 24, 168
Inquisitive minds – 154
Insight – 310
Inspiration – 203

J

Jealousy – 165, 281
Jigsaw – 157
Journey of the cross – 328
Judging others – 53, 104, 147, 182, 285
Judging success – 142

K

Kindness – 288, 304
Kindness to self – 286
Know self – 112, 275

L

Lashing out – 212
Laughter – 346
Learning – 31, 248, 301
Lie – 178, 230, 269, 325
Life – 244
Life, a day in – 121
Life & imperfection – 1
Life journey – 156, 169

Life teachers – 146
Limitations – 241, 284, 316
Listening – 82, 266
Living in the moment – 67
Loneliness, aloneness – 58
Loss – 250
Loss & Grief – 277
Lost opportunity – 358
Love – 102, 162, 270, 360
Love thy neighbour – 38
Lucky country – 232

M

Making a Difference – 253
Making a Mark – 341
Masks – 117, 214, 340
Meditation – 352
Meaningful life – 259
Memories – 224, 260, 307, 342
Mental Health – 361
Miracles – 219, 326
Mistakes – 174, 242, 349
Misery – 40, 114
Misunderstanding – 345
Morning – 329
Mother Mary, in my life – 317
Mothers love – 330
Motivation – 166, 363

N

Needs – 189
Negative outcomes – 80
Negative thoughts – 108
New Paths – 73
New places – 89
New Year's Resolution – 246
Nicknames – 211
Night Sky – 347
No – 115, 291

O

Optimist – 69

P

Participation in life – 27
Past, the – 11
Paths – 60, 72, 254
Patience – 3, 48, 265, 320
Pedestal – 68
Perfection – 136, 177
Personal journey – 355
Possessions – 20
Possibilities – 171
Positive – 201
Potential – 109, 255, 362
Poverty of spirit – 37
Poverty – 42
Prayer – 76, 93, 205, 274, 279, 303, 314
Praise – 220
Preferences – 258
Procrastination – 6, 271
Promise – 135

Q

Question & Answer – 12
Quite time – 139

R

Racism – 130, 217
Rainbow – 181
Reflection – 124
Regrets – 327
Relationships – 95
Respect – 50, 134, 282
Response – 84
Right path – 111
Right time – 164

S

Sacrifice – 188
Seeing fully – 79
Seeing things differently – 148, 227
Self-belief – 100, 315
Self-esteem – 138, 245
Setbacks – 186
Sharing – 29, 150
Sickness – 91
Silence – 309
Speaking out – 35
Special – 145
Success – 204
Suffering – 25, 30, 292, 294, 359
Suffering & Compassion – 337
Sunday drive – 261
Supporting others – 338

T

Take for granted – 222
Tears – 45
Thanks – 160, 276, 290
Thanks & sorry – 133
Thank you Mother Mary – 365
Time – 34, 46, 126, 295, 333
Tough times – 118, 119, 313
Tragedy – 308
Treated, how you would like – 161
Trials – 318
Trust – 238
Truth – 22, 41, 59, 77
Truth & Faith – 293

U

Uniqueness – 43, 272, 306

V

Viewpoint – 144
Violence – 21

W

Weeds – 92, 129
Welcome the morning – 52
When to keep quiet – 123
Why me – 70
Words of kindness – 223
Worry – 256
Wrongdoing – 247

www.ingramcontent.com/pod-product-compliance
Lightning Source LLC
Chambersburg PA
CBHW040315170426
43196CB00020B/2932